The Complete Learn Hebrew For Beginners Book (3 in 1)

Master Reading, Writing, and Speaking in Hebrew With This Integrated Textbook and Workbook

Worldwide Nomad

CONTENTS

Hebrew Grammar Workbook and Textbook For Beginners

Hebrew Phrasebook for Beginners

Hebrew Short Stories for Language Learners

Hebrew Grammar Workbook and Textbook For *Beginners*

Learn Hebrew With Essential, Easy to Understand Lessons

Index

- **Dagesh:** In this section, the learner discovers the significance of the "Dagesh", a diacritic mark indicating consonant doubling or strengthening in Hebrew, and its role in clarifying pronunciation and grammatical structure. Through comprehensive exploration and practical examples, they gain insight into the impact of Dagesh on the phonetic precision and morphology of Hebrew words.

Chapter 4: The Article

- **Indefinite and Definite Article in Hebrew:** The "Indefinite and Definite Article in Hebrew" section provides insight into the usage and distinctions between the indefinite article "a" and the definite article "the" in Hebrew, elaborating their impact on sentence structure and meaning.

Chapter 5: The Noun

- **Gender:** The "Gender in Hebrew" section explores the grammatical intricacies of assigning gender to nouns, discussing the linguistic nuances associated with masculine and feminine classifications.

- **Pluralization:** The "Pluralization in Hebrew" section delves into the methods and patterns used to form plural nouns in Hebrew, emphasizing the impact on both vowels and consonants.

- **Case:** The "Noun Case in Hebrew" section explores the concept of grammatical case in nouns, discussing how cases, such as the construct state, affect the forms and relationships between nouns.

Chapter 6: The Adjective

- **Comparison of Adjectives:** The "Comparison of Adjectives" section explores the nuanced world of adjective comparison in Hebrew, delving into the various forms and structures used to express degrees of comparison. Through detailed analysis and practical examples, gain insight into how Hebrew handles comparatives and superlatives, enhancing the learner's ability to describe and compare in the Hebrew language.

- **Numerals:** The "Numerals" section uncovers the diverse forms of numeral expression in the Hebrew language. Through comprehensive exploration and practical examples, it allows the learner to delve into the cardinal and ordinal numbers, mastering the art of counting and numbering in Hebrew texts and conversations.

Chapter 7: Pronouns

- **Personal Pronouns:** The "Personal Pronouns" section dives into the essential role of personal pronouns in Hebrew, exploring their nuanced forms and functions in communication. From singular to plural, first person to third person, unravel the complexities of how personal pronouns express subjects and objects in Hebrew sentences.

- **Demonstrative Pronouns:** The "Demonstrative Pronouns" section uncovers the essential role of demonstrative pronouns in Hebrew, unveiling their crucial role in indicating proximity and specificity.

- **The Relative Pronoun:** The "Relative Pronoun" section navigates the intricate landscape of the relative pronoun in Hebrew, uncovering its pivotal role in connecting dependent clauses to their antecedents. The learner will explore how relative pronouns establish relationships and provide essential context within complex sentences.

- **Interrogative Pronouns:** The "Interrogative Pronouns" section provides an in-depth exploration of these pronoun types, highlighting how they indicate proximity, association, and inquiry in the Hebrew language. Unraveling their significance in forming questions and seeking information. From "mi" to "mah", the learner will delve into the diverse forms and functions of interrogative pronouns, essential for inquiry and clarification in Hebrew communication.

Chapter 8: Prepositions

- **Overview of Hebrew Prepositions:** The "Overview of Hebrew Prepositions" section provides a comprehensive understanding of prepositions in Hebrew, discussing their role in indicating relationships between elements in a sentence and their influence on word meaning.

Chapter 9: Conjunctions

- **Overview of Hebrew Conjunction:** The "Overview of Hebrew Conjunctions" section explores the function and types of conjunctions in Hebrew, emphasizing their role in connecting words, phrases, or clauses within sentences.

Chapter 10: Hebrew Verb System

- **Overview of Hebrew Verb System:** The "Overview of Hebrew Verb System" section provides a comprehensive insight into the structure of the Hebrew verb system, covering conjugations, tenses, and binyanim, emphasizing their crucial role in expressing actions and states.

- **Conjugations in Hebrew:** "Verb Conjugation in Hebrew" explores the intricate system of modifying verb forms to indicate tense, mood, aspect, and subject agreement, employing root letters and vowel patterns for various conjugations. Through structured rules and patterns, learners navigate the complexities of Hebrew verbs to express precise actions and states.

Introduction

Welcome to the world of the Hebrew language, as this book opens the doors to learning about one of the most influential languages in history. It covers an immense range of topics that will help you learn everything related to the Hebrew language in daily subjects. The Hebrew language, the language of the Bible and ancient Jewish culture, captivates hearts with its great history and rich structure. This book is your companion on your journey to explore and learn this language, from the basics to advanced language challenges.

What distinguishes this book:

This book is not just an educational guide, but rather your travel companion that takes you step by step into the world of the Hebrew language. Here are some points that distinguish this book:

1. **Strong foundation in grammar:** This book will give you a deep understanding of the grammatical and linguistic rules of the Hebrew language, which will enable you to build understandable sentences and express with confidence.
2. **Practical exercises:** In this book you will find many practical exercises that will help you apply what you have learned and enhance your language skills.
3. **It allows you to learn something new every day:** This book will provide you with daily lessons inspired by your daily life, where every day you will learn new vocabulary and phrases to improve your Hebrew language in an effective way.

Learning Hebrew is not just a challenge to achieve, but an exciting journey in exploring a rich culture and connecting with an extended history. This book aims to make learning Hebrew an enjoyable and inspiring experience, as it introduces you to the basics in an easy and simple manner.

This introduction is a guide to help you get started in Hebrew and polish your basic grammar, spelling, punctuation, and vocabulary skills. Good luck – and **most importantly, enjoy yourself!**

Chapter 1
Introduction to the Hebrew Alphabet

In-depth Study of Consonant Sounds

The Hebrew alphabet is structured in a unique way. It follows a right-to-left writing direction, a characteristic that sets it apart from left-to-right written languages. Given that Hebrew belongs to the Semitic language family, the appearance of the Hebrew alphabet may look different from what you're used to. Unlike most languages, the Hebrew alphabet does not have vowels. Instead, it contains 22 consonants. Hebrew has a separate writing system for vowels, which we will explore later in this learning journey.

The table below lists the Hebrew alphabet letters along with their name in Hebrew. You will also find an approximate English pronunciation for each Hebrew letter. It's important to note that certain letters, such as ח lack a direct English equivalent. You must learn to familiarize yourself with the Hebrew alphabet and practice how to pronounce Hebrew letters correctly.

Name	Sign	Sound	Corresponding English Letter
Aleph	א	sounds like *a* as in English *at*	A
Beth [1]	ב	sounds like *b* as in English *bar* if with dagesh, and sounds like *v* as in English *van* if not	B
Gimel	ג	sounds like *g* as in English *good*	G
Daleth	ד	sounds like *d* as in English *dad*	D
Hey	ה	sounds like *h* as in English *hot*	H
Vav	ו	sounds like *v* as in English *van*	V
Zayn	ז	sounds like *z* as in English *zoo*	Z
Cheth	ח	doesn't exist in English, but sounds like *ch* in *Bach*	CH
Teth	ט	sounds like *t* as in English *tea*	T
Yod	י	sounds like *y* as in English *yell*	Y

Kaf [1 2]	כ/ך	sounds like *c/k* as in English *cat* if with dagesh, and sounds like *ch* in *Bach* if not	K
Lamed	ל	sounds like *l* as in English *laugh*	L
Mem [2]	מ/ם	sounds like *m* as in English *mom*	M
Nun [2]	נ/ן	sounds like *n* as in English *nap*	N
Samech	ס	sounds like *s* as in English *sad*	S
Ayin	ע	doesn't exist in English, sounds similar to a glottal *a* sound	A
Pey [1 2]	פ/ף	sounds like *p* as in English *pet* if with dagesh, and sounds like *f* in English *far* if not	P
Tsadi [2]	צ/ץ	sounds like *ts* as in English *nuts*	TS
Kuf	ק	sounds like *k* as in English *cake*	K
Reysh	ר	sounds like *r* as in French *merci*	R
Sin [3]	שׂ	sounds like *s* as in English *snake*	S
Shin [3]	שׁ	sounds like *sh* as in English *sharp*	SH
Taf	ת	sounds like *t* as in English *tap*	T

Remarks:

1. These letters marked with 1 are pronounced differently when marked by a *dagesh*[1]. These letters are three and they are: בּ, כּ, פּ. Note that whenever בּ, כּ or פּ open a word, they are automatically

[1] Dagesh is a diacritical mark which serves the purpose of doubling the letter.

read with a dagesh. בּ makes a *b* sound instead of *v*. כּ makes a *k* sound instead of guttural *ch*. Lastly, פּ makes a *p* sound instead of *f*.

2. These letters marked with 2 change shape when they appear at the end of a word. These letters are five and they are: Kaf - ך/כ, Mem - ם/מ, Nun - ן/נ, Pey – ף/פ, Tsadi - ץ/צ.
3. The letter (שׁ) marked with 3 can sound like *s* or like *sh* depending on the dot it has above it. If the dot is on the left side, it sounds like *s*, if it's on the right side, it sounds like *sh*.
4. Hebrew words are written from right to left, not as in English from left to right. Therefore, if we wish to write down the Hebrew letters for a word in which the consonants are in the order b r ch in English letters, we write in Hebrew ברח, the first letter being at the right hand of the word.
5. Aleph represents the catch in the breath heard in English between two vowels in a word like "re-inforce." You may regard it as a mute letter. However, in transliterating (which is writing out the Hebrew letters in the corresponding letters of the English Alphabet) Aleph is usually represented by '.
6. Ayin ע is a difficult sound and may be taken by the beginner as a mute letter. It is represented in transliteration by '.
7. English does not have a letter that can be compared to Cheth ח. The final *ch* in *Bach* represents the sound fairly well. You will not find that sound at the beginning of a word in English, but it is frequently placed in Hebrew.
8. Tsadi is to be pronounced as *ts*. Many Hebrew speakers prefer to pronounce this letter as an emphatic s, like a double s.

Final Letters

As we previously mentioned, in Hebrew there are five letters that change shape when they appear at the end of a word: ך (Kaf Sofit), ם (Mem Sofit), ן (Nun Sofit), ף (Pey Sofit), and ץ (Tsadi Sofit). When these letters appear at the end of a word, they take on a unique, final form. This visual distinction adds a layer of sophistication to the written Hebrew language.

The use of final letters enhances the visual harmony of the written script. Whether in sacred texts or everyday writings, the appearance of a final letter marks the end of a word, contributing to the overall aesthetic appeal of the Hebrew language.

In terms of pronunciation, final letters are silent when positioned at the end of a word. Unlike their non-final counterparts, which carry distinct sounds, final letters add a visual marker without altering the spoken form. For example, the final form of "כ" (Kaf) is "ך," pronounced "kaf sofit."

While final letters are silent, practicing their pronunciation in the context of complete words aids in developing a natural and fluent reading style. The awareness of the subtle phonetic nuances enhances overall language proficiency.

Letter	Non-Final Form	Final Form
Kaf	כ	ך
Mem	מ	ם
Nun	נ	ן
Pey	פ	ף
Tsadi	צ	ץ

Dagesh - Attention has been called to the point in the body of 3 letters: בּ (Beth), כּ (Kaf), פּ (Pey). Sometimes they are written without the dagesh, and then there is a change in the pronunciation. Beth with the Dagesh is pronounced like "b" in "bind," but without the dagesh it is pronounced like "v" in "vine". Kaf with the Dagesh is pronounced like "k" in "kind", without the dagesh is pronounced like "ch" in "Bach". Pey with Dagesh is pronounced like "p" in "pain", but is pronounced like "ph" in the word "philosopher" without it.

Remarks:

1. You might have noticed the resemblance between some of the letters of the Hebrew Alphabet. For example, Beth has a similar shape to Kaf, but note that Beth ב is not rounded like Kaf כ.
2. Gimel ג and Nun נ also might resemble each other.
3. Sometimes Daleth ד and Reysh ר are confused; but you can notice that Reysh is rounded, unlike Daleth.
4. Note that there is a short upright line at the left of Hey ה, while both the upright lines in Cheth ח are of the same size. Note the open space between the left upright stroke in Hey and the top horizontal line. There is no such space in Cheth.
5. You can also notice the difference between Vav ו, Zayin ז, and Yod י. Vav comes down to the line, but Yod does not. The short line at the top of Zayin goes beyond the upright to the right, but in Vav we don't have such a thing.

Exercise 1:

1. Which letter in the Hebrew alphabet represents the sound "B"?

a) ב
b) ג
c) ד
d) ה

2. What is the name of the Hebrew letter "כ"?

a) Kaf
b) Bet

c) Gimel
d) Tet

3. What sound does the Hebrew letter “ש” represent?

a) F
b) T
c) Sh
d) K

4. The Hebrew letter “צ” is equivalent to which English letter?

a) Tz
b) Z
c) S
d) Ch

5. What is the last letter of the Hebrew alphabet?

a) ר
b) ש
c) ת
d) ק

6. Which Hebrew letter is used to represent the “V” sound?

a) ע
b) ה
c) ג
d) ו

7. The Hebrew letter “ז” represents the sound “...............”.

8. The name of the Hebrew letter “פ” is “...............”.

9. The Hebrew letter “ט” is equivalent to the English letter “...............”.

10. The sound represented by the Hebrew letter “מ” is “...............”.

11. The final form of the Hebrew letter “נ” is “...............”.

12. The Hebrew letter “ר” is pronounced as “...............”.

13. The letter "ס" in Hebrew corresponds to the English letter "...............".

14. The Hebrew letter "כ" has a final form, which is "...............".

15. The sound represented by the Hebrew letter "ל" is "...............".

Chapter 2
Vowels (Nikud)

As previously mentioned, the Hebrew alphabet does not have vowels. Instead, the vowels in Hebrew are represented by small strokes and points, which are placed either below, above, or even in the center of the consonants to which their sounds severally pertain.

These marks, which are also called Nikud, are ten in number, of which five are long and five are short. Please find the following table which represents their names, signs, and power:

1. Long Vowels

Names	Sign	Power
Kamets Gadol	xָ	*a* as in *hall*
Tseri	xֵ	*a* as in *hate*
Chireq Gadol	יִx	*i* as in *pique*
Cholam	וֹx	*o* as in *go*
Shureq	וּx	*oo* as in *moon*

2. Short Vowels

Names	Sign	Power
Pattach	xַ	*a* as in *hat*
Segol	xֶ	*e* as in *met*
Chireq Qatan	xִ	*i* as in *pin*
Kibbuts	xֻ	*u* as in *pull*
Kamets Chateph	xָ	*o* as in *not*

Remarks:

1. Please note that the vowels signs below have been magnified to help you learn them. They will usually be smaller in actual Hebrew texts.
2. The consonants are always sounded before the vowels, not after them. For example: בָּ is sounded as ba, not ab.
3. The names of the Nikud signs are derived, mostly, from the position of the organs of speech in pronouncing them. Thus, קָמֵץ Kamets signifies "contraction" (i.e., of the mouth); פַּתַּח Pattah, "opening" (i.e., of the mouth); קִבּוּץ Kibbuts "compression" (i.e., of the lips). סגול Segol, a cluster of grapes, derives its name from its form. קמץ חטף Kamets Chateph is merely the Hebrew expression for Kamets short, which is called so to distinguish it from simple Kamets.

The Long Vowels

This section will discuss what are known as the long vowel sounds in Hebrew writing. These five long vowel sounds will be expressed as follows:

(1) Kamets Gadol (ָx): In Hebrew, the vowel sound "a" is written beneath the preceding consonant. The syllable "ba" - would therefore be represented as בָּ.

In order to distinguish this Nikud (vowel sign) from Kamets Chateph, which has the same shape but sounds like a short "o", this point is sometimes referred to as "Kamets Gadol", not just "Kamets". P.S. There will be some hints on how to tell them apart in a later section. There is a lot of variation in how Kamets is pronounced among Jews and Hebrew scholars from various countries. Jews from Spain and Portugal, for example, pronounce it as "a" in "far", e.g., בָּרָא will be pronounced as "bah-rah". While Jews from Germany and Poland will pronounce it as "o" in "bone," for example, "bo-ro".

P.S. In final Kaf ך Kamets is not written underneath as usual, but in the bosom, thus ךָ.

Examples

אָ: a - בָּ: ba - דָ: da - נָא: na - מָא: ma - קָה: qah

שָׁה: Shah - לָךְ: laka

(2) Tseri (ֵx): The vowel sign for the sound "ë" is called "Tseri". It's represented beneath the preceding consonant. The Hebrew word for "a son", "bën," is thus written בֵּן.

Examples

אֵ: ë - תֵּ: të - מֵ: më - גֵּ: gë - רֵא: rë

פֵּה: pëh - שֵׁה: shëh

(3) Chireq Gadol (ִיx): The vowel sign for the sound "i" is called "Chireq Gadol". It's represented in Hebrew by ִx written under the consonant, then preceded with the letter "Yod". "Yod" then loses its value as a consonant. This has an English equivalent in the word "Bay", for example, where the "Y" has lost its value and its sound as a consonant. The Hebrew word for "to me", "לִי" is spelled with this sound.

Note that the dot beneath the consonant alone is called "Chireq" or "Chireq Qatan" and it's one of the short vowels that we'll talk about later. This means that the presence of the Yod י is the main mark of distinction between "Chireq Gadol" and "Chireq Qatan". Accordingly, דִּיל is pronounced "deel", and דִּל is pronounced "dil".

Examples

בִּי: bee - דִּין: deen - גִּיל: geel - מִין: meen

זִיף: zeef - רִיק: reeq

(4) Cholam (אֹ): There are two methods to represent the sound o: either with or without the help of a consonant, the consonant here would be the letter "Vav". However, the "Vav" is frequently omitted. For example, the sound for the word "coal" is written in two ways, either קֹל or קוֹל. We transliterate both ways as "qōl". Also, the word "Yil-mod", which could be written as יִלְמֹד or יִלְמוֹד.

To summarize, this means without the help of the "Vav", the vowel sign "Cholam" is a dot above the consonant. If "Vav" is used, the dot appears above the "Vav" itself.

It's also worth mentioning that, in some places, this might not be the case. If the "Vav" has a vowel under it, it should be pronounced as a consonant. It's like the "Vav" gets back its lost powers as a consonant. For example, the word "Ye-ho-vah" "יְהוָֹה'.

Examples

בֹּו: bo - דּוֹם: dom - כֹּל: kol - שֹׁן: son

חֹשׁ: hosh - הֹשֶׂה: ho-seh

(5) Shureq (אוּ): In Hebrew, the vowel sound "u" is represented with the vowel sign "אוּ" after the consonant to which its sound belongs. However, it should not be confused with the Dageshed "Vav" which looks exactly the same. Shureq and Dageshed Vav are different in that Shureq never has a vowel under it, while Dageshed Vav always has a Sheva[2], it looks like this under the letter Alef for example: אְ) or a vowel beneath it, except when Shureq follows it. As an example, קוּם s pronounced "qum", but קִוֵּם is pronounced qiv-vam.

When a word starts with the Shureq, it is pronounced as u = oo. For example, וּמִי is pronounced "u-mi", not "vu-mi".

Examples

גּוּ: gu - לוּן: lun - רוּב: ruv - רוּבוּ: ru-vu

נוּן: nun - רִוָּהוּ: riv-va-hu - רִוּוּ: riv-vu

[2] Sheva is a mark placed under a letter that does not have a vowel, it looks like this under the letter Alef for example: אְ.

The Short Vowels

This section will discuss what are known as the short vowel sounds in Hebrew writing. These five short vowel sounds will be expressed as follows:

(1) Pattach (ַx): In Hebrew, the vowel-sound ă is represented by "ַ" written under the preceding consonant. This vowel-sign is called "Pathach". The Hebrew term for "a mountain," "hăr," is thus spelled הַר.

Almost generally, Pattach is a short vowel; nevertheless, it is long before a quiescent, as in לִקְרַאת liq-reth, not liq-răth," and before a Guttural with a Dagesh, as in "בַּהֵל be-hel".

The primary characteristic of Pattach is its frequent usage under the gutturals ,ע ,ח ,ה when final, for euphonic purposes. In this instance, the Pattach is sounded before the letter it is positioned beneath, in contrary to usual analogy. Accordingly, רוּחַ is pronounced ru- ăhh, not ru-hhă, and גָּבוֹ הַ is pronounced ga-vo- ăh, not ga-vo-hă. In this case, Pattach is called "Pattach Furtive". Pattach Furtive appears under all gutturals, with the exception of א that never accepts it.

Examples

טַל: tăl - רַת: răth - רוּעַ: ru-ă - רֵעַ: re-ă

שָׁמוּעַ: sha-mu-ă - נוּחַ: nu-ăhh

(2) Segol (ֶx): The vowel sign for the sound "ĕ" is called "Segol". It's represented in Hebrew by ֶx written under the consonant. Despite being categorised as a short vowel, Segol turns long in the following instances:

1. When being in a simple syllable, for example, כֶּסֶף which is pronounced kë-sĕph, and מֶלֶךְ which is pronounced më-lĕch;

2. Before the quiescent letters א ,ה ,י ; as מִקְנֶה which is pronounced as miq-nëh, not miq-nĕh;

3. Before a Guttural with a Dagesh, for example, אֶחָיו which is pronounced ë-hhâv for אַחָיו ă-hhâv.

In these three cases, Segol is to be sounded like Tseri.

Examples

בֶל: vĕl - מֶת: mĕt - בֶּטֶן: bë-tĕn - נֶפֶשׁ: në-phĕsh

מֹרֶה: mö-rëh - עֹלֶה: ö-lëh

(3) Chireq Qatan (ִx): Please refer to "Chireq Gadol" in the Long Vowels section.

(4) Kibbuts (ֻx): The vowel sign for the sound "ŭ" is called "Kibbuts". Kibbuts is frequently used as a substitute for Shureq; for example, קֻטָל for קָטוּל, and קֻמוֹ for קוּמוֹ. In this instance, it's a long vowel and it's called "Kibbuts Vicarious".

Examples

אֻב: ŭv - לֻם: lŭm - גָּזֻל: ga-zŭl - לֻקָּה: lŭq-qah

כֻּלָּם: kŭl-lam - כְּרֻבִים: kĕ-rŭ-vim

(5) Kamets Chateph (ָx): This vowel agrees in form with Kamets Gadol. Meanwhile Kamets Gadol is pronounced as â, Kamets Chateph is pronounced as ŏ. The main rule for distinguishing them is that Kamets Chateph is uaually followed by a Sheva.[3] For example, חָכְמָה is pronounced as hhŏch-mâh.

Examples

חָכְמָה: hhŏch-mâh - קָרְבָּן: qŏr-bŏn - כָּל: Kŏl

Remarks:

1. Soon, the learner will be able to distinguish between the signs that indicate long and short vowels. It suffices to know that a vowel is typically long in an open syllable and short in a closed one. A syllable is considered closed if it ends in a consonantal sound, and open if it ends in a vowel sound.
2. Unless you are certain that it is Kamets in a certain word is Kamets Chateph, it is a fairly good working rule to pronounce it as Kamets Gadol.

Exercise 2:

1. What is the term for the diacritic marks used to represent vowels in Hebrew?

   a) Nikud
   b) Dagesh
   c) Sheva
   d) Segol

2. Which vowel point is represented by a dot placed under the letter?

   a) Segol
   b) Kamatz

[3] Sheva is a mark placed under a letter that does not have a vowel, it looks like this under the letter Alef for example: אְ.

c) Chireq Qatan
d) Shureq

3. What vowel point is used to represent the long “i” sound in Hebrew?

a) Kamatz
b) Patach
c) Chireq
d) Chireq Gadol

4. Which vowel point is used to represent the “oo” sound in Hebrew?

a) Kamatz
b) Shureq
c) Cholam
d) Segol

5. The vowel “ָ” is called “...............” in Hebrew.

6. The vowel “ִ” is known as “...............” in Hebrew.

7. The vowel “ֵ” is pronounced as “...............” in Hebrew.

8. The vowel “ֶ” is known as “...............” in Hebrew.

9. The vowel “ֻ” represents the sound “...............” in Hebrew.

10. The vowel “ַ” is pronounced as “...............” in Hebrew.

Chapter 3
Syllables, Sheva, and Dagesh

Syllables in Hebrew

A Syllable in Hebrew can be either a simple syllable or a mixed one. A simple syllable is one that ends in a vowel sound, with or without a quiescent letter. Examples of such a simple syllable that ends without a quiescent: בָּ, נָ, רֵ, and examples of such a simple syllable that ends with a quiescent: בָּא, לֹא, מִי.

A mixed syllable is one that ends with a consonant sound, like in the words אֵל, מוֹל, כּוֹל. Thus, the first syllable in words like: מֶלֶךְ, לָמַד, בַּיִת is simple, whereas the second syllable is mixed.

Before moving on, it will be important to explain the uses of Sheva, which are fundamental to the skill of reading Hebrew once a student has mastered the letters and vowels that are closely linked to the many applications of the Sheva.

Sheva

In Hebrew, two consonants at the beginning of a syllable do not combine into one sound, unlike in English terms like brand, grade, bled, and so on. In order to prevent this, the Hebrew language uses a very short "half-vowel", presented by the symbol (:). This half-vowel is vocally equivalent to the "e" in reckon, and its sound falls between the two consonant letters. As a result, the terms above would be pronounced as gerade, berand, beled, and so on. Sheva is the name of this "e" sound in between the two consonants; it is primarily used in euphonic contexts because it is not a syllable in and of itself. Therefore, even though they might sound like dissyllables, פְּרִי, בְּנִי, and פְּקֹד are all regarded as purely monosyllables. However, some linguists question this.

The Sheva comes in two forms: simple and composite. The simple Sheva (:) can be placed under any consonant, with the exception of the gutturals, which occasionally accept it. The composite Sheva, with a few uncommon exceptions, are solely found beneath the Gutturals. The reason why the composite Sheva is named so because it's made up of a simple Sheva combined with one of the short vowels. Hence, there are three of forms of the composite Sheva, the following table shows their names, forms, and sounds:

Hebrew Names	Names in English	Form	Sounds
חָטֵף פַּתַח	Hateph Pattach	xֲ	"*a*" as in *lark*
חָטֵף סְגוֹל	Hateph Segol	xֱ	"*e*" as in *memory*
חָטֵף קָמֵץ	Hateph Kamets	xֳ	"*oa*" as in *boat*

Sheva also has two kinds of power: it's either vocal or silent. The learner will be able to identify when any of the two scenarios is true by using the guidelines that follow:

1) Vocal Sheva: Sheva is vocal and sounded when:

a) At the beginning of a word; for example, לְבָב which is pronounced as le-vav, קְטֹל which is sounded as qe-tol.
b) At the beginning of a syllable, in the midst of a word; following a long vowel (if unaccented), for example, קוֹטְלָה which is pronounced qo-te-lah; or following another Sheva, as in יִלְמְד ו yil-me-du; or under a Dageshed letter, as in שִׁבְּרוּ. This latter situation is equal to two separate Shevas.
c) Under a letter that has Dagesh forte applied, which is typically (though not always) the case when a letter is repeated, such as in הַלְלוּ = הַלְלוּ which is pronounced hal-Ie-lu.
d) Also, when the composite Shevas start a syllable; for example, אֲזָרִים, יַעֲשֶׂה, they are always vocal.

2) Silent Sheva: Sheva is silent when:

a) Following a short vowel in a mixed syllable; for example, יִקְטֹל which is pronounced yĭq-tol, מַלְכָּה which is pronounced măl-kah.
b) In an accented syllable, following a long vowel; for example, שֹׁבְנָה shov-nah, and תִּלְמֹדְנָה til-mod-nah. In this instance, the syllable is rendered mixed simply by the accentuation. Otherwise, it would be a simple syllable, and the Sheva would be vocal, שֹׁבְנָה would be pronounced sho-ve-nah and תִּלְמֹדְנָה would be pronounced til-mo-de-nah. Therefore, it is not always possible to determine the genuine character of the Sheva without understanding the accentual system (will discuss it in a later section).
c) When two Shevas meet at the end of a word, both are always silent; for example: קַמְתְּ qămt, and יָשַׁנְתְּ yâ-shănt.

Generally speaking, any movable letter[4] that does not have another point associated with it needs to have a Sheva. When it comes to the quiescent letters, or those that coalesce with a preceding vowel, the situation is different; they do not accept Sheva, for example, רֵאשׁ , בֵּין, יֹאמַר.

Sheva is always implied rather than expressed at the end of words; for example, קָם = קָםְ, לָמַד = לָמַדְ. Only one exception in the final Kaf, as Sheva is written in this case, such as דֶּרֶךְ, סָמַךְ.

As was previously mentioned, when a final syllable ends in two consonants, Sheva is expressed beneath both, as in the case of לָמַדְתְּ la-matht and נָתַנְתְּ na-thant.

The gutturals always take Sheva simple when they fall at the end of a syllable, except for this case, they require the composite Shevas as mentioned before. Thus, it's יֶחְדַל yĕhh-dăl, not ye-hhe-dăl, and שָׁמַעְתִּי shâ-mă-ti, not shâ-mă-ă-ti.

[4] A moveable letter is any pronounced letter. This term is used to differentiate between such letter and quiescent letters.

Dagesh

As we have mentioned before, Dagesh is a diacritical mark which is inserted into the bosom of a letter (בּ). Dagesh serves two important purposes:

1) It doubles the letter, for example, קִטְטֵל = קִטֵּל qit-tel, יְלַמְמֵד = יְלַמֵּד ye-lam-med. In this case, it's called "Dagesh Forte". Consonants with Dagesh Forte combined with Sheva are pronounced like two consonants with a simple Sheva in the middle of a word. Hence, דַּבְּרוּ is pronounced as though it was written דַבְבְרוּ dab-be-ru, and מִמֶּנּוּ which is pronounced as if it was written מִמְמֶנוּ mim-me-nu, where the first sheva is silent and the second one is vocal.

2) It removes the aspirate from the Begad Kephat letters[5], as in מִדְבָּר which is pronounced mid-bar; in contrast, in the absence of the Dagesh, מִדְבָר mid-var. In this case, it's known as "Dagesh Lene".

Remarks:

1. The primary difference between Dagesh Forte and Dagesh Lene is that the former never appears in the first or last letter of a word, and it's always preceded by a short vowel right before it; examples of Dagesh Forte are: לִמֵּד ⊠lim-med, יְקַטֵּל ye-qat-tel.
2. Dagesh Forte can appear with every letter, with the exception of the gutturals א, ה, ח, ע and ר, which is similar to the gutturals in many ways and shares with the many characteristics. Due to the inherent incapability of these letters to be duplicated, whenever they would get Dagesh, it would be omitted; the omission is made up for by prolonging the preceding vowel, as in the case of זֵעֵק for זִעֵק, בֵּרֵךְ for בִּרֵךְ, and בָּרֵךְ for בֵּרֵךְ.
3. Dagesh Lene belongs to the Aspirates (Begad Kephat בגד כפת). It serves for the purpose of announcing that these letters should be pronounced without aspiration. As a result, Beth with the Dagesh is pronounced like "b" in "bind," but without the dagesh it is pronounced like "v" in "vine". Kaf with the Dagesh is pronounced like "k" in "kind", without the dagesh is pronounced like "ch" in "Bach". Pey with Dagesh is pronounced like "p" in "pain", etc.
4. Sometimes Dagesh Forte also appears in the Aspirates. Its impact is not only that it causes reduplication, but it's sometimes similar to Dagesh Lene's in that it removes the aspirate sound, as in the case of שַׁבָּת shab-bat, for example.

[5] We have mentioned the Begad Kephat בגד כפת letters before, it's is the name given to a phenomenon of lenition affecting the non-emphatic stop consonants when they are preceded by a vowel and not geminated. These 6 letters בגד כפת has only 3 that still follow this rule in modern Hebrew, which are בכפ, the other 3 letters גדת are no longer following the Begad Kephat rule in Modern Hebrew. So simply, when a Dagesh is placed in the body of the 3 letters: בּ (Beth), כּ (Kaf), פּ (Pey) they change in the pronunciation. Beth with the Dagesh is pronounced like "b" in "bind," but without the dagesh it is pronounced like "v" in "vine". Kaf with the Dagesh is pronounced like "k" in "kind", without the dagesh is pronounced like "ch" in "Bach". Pey with Dagesh is pronounced like "p" in "pain", but is pronounced like "ph" in the word "philosopher" without it.

Exercise 3:

1. When does the Dagesh appear in the Hebrew letter "כ" (Kaf)?

   a) Always
   b) Never
   c) After a vowel
   d) At the beginning of a word or after certain prefixes

2. How many types of Sheva are there in Hebrew?

   a) One
   b) Two
   c) Three
   d) Four

3. Which of the following letters cannot take a Dagesh?

   a) ד
   b) ג
   c) ת
   d) א

4. The Dagesh is a diacritic mark in Hebrew that indicates consonant "..............." or removes the aspirate from the Begad Kephat letters.

Chapter 4
The Article

In Hebrew, there is no such thing as an indefinite article, unlike the English "a" or "an". "A city", for example, is עִיר which is pronounced as ir.

Unlike our "The", the Definite Article is just a letter that is inserted at the start of the word to which it is attached rather than as a stand-alone word. Its typical form is הַ (hă), with the following letter doubled. As a result, יוֹם pronounced as yom is "a day", but "the day" pronounced as hăy-yom is actually "הַיּוֹם" which has the symbol for a double letter "dagesh". The following consonant should be doubled by Dagesh to represent the Definite Article, unless there is a good cause to do differently.

The Definite Article in Hebrew is indiscriminately prefixed to nouns of all genders, numbers, and cases, as well as to participles and adjectives. This corresponds to the English definite article "The"; for example, דְּבָרִים words, הַדְּבָרִים the words - שֶׁמֶשׁ sun, הַשֶּׁמֶשׁ the sun.

When it comes to uses, it should be noted that the Definite Article serves two purposes:

1. Marking the subject as known already, either from general consent or from the context, for example: הָאוֹר the light; and
2. To impress upon the hearer's or reader's mind the unique quality, nature, or character of the subject to which it refers, for example: הָאֱלֹהִים the real or true God; הַדּוֹב a specific bear.

The Definite Article's appropriate vowel is Pattah הַ, and a Dagesh appears in the following letter, for example: הַתּוֹרָה the law, הַנָּהָר the river. However, it's assumed by the Hebrew linguists that the subsequent Dagesh in this instance is compensatory of what was omitted or of some kind of assimilation; as if the article's original form was הַל, which corresponds to the Arabic אַל. However, there is scant or no evidence for this. The form of the article is the same in the oldest examples of the language that have been preserved for us in the Scriptures as it is in the writings of Ezra, written several hundred years later, showing no signs of the Lamed. The likelihood that the Arabs introduced the Lamed is far higher than the likelihood that the Hebrews rejected it.

Regarding the Dagesh that follows, it is reasonable to assume that makes it necessary that the next letter be doubled in order to finish the syllable that the Article starts.

However, the Article takes on a long vowel when it comes before a Guttural (which does not accept the Dagesh, as we explained before). This can be either Kamets, for example הָעַיִן the eye, הָראשׁ the head, or Segol, particularly before Kamets, as הֶהָרִים the mountains, and הֶעָנָן the cloud.

The Article generally disappears when one of the prepositions בְּ, לְ, כְּ comes before it. But, in this case, the Article always leaves its appropriate vowel under the preposition to take its place and as a sign that the Article was there, for example: בַּשָּׁמַיִם for בְּהַשָּׁמַיִם.

Remarks:

1. Please note that sometimes the Pattah stays unchanged even though not being followed by a Dagesh; for example, הַחֹדֶשׁ the month, and הַיְאֹר the river. However, these are exceptional cases.

2. There are few occasions where the Article is still there even though it is a preposition comes before it; these are appropriately regarded as exceptions to the rule, for example, לְהָעָם, and כְּהַיּוֹם.
3. When the Article precedes the following words and a few more, it lengthens the short vowel in their first letter: עַם, הָעָם - צַר, הַצָּר - הַר, הָהָר - עַם, הָעָם - אֶרֶץ, הָאָרֶץ.

Exercise 4:

1. What is the Hebrew definite article?

a) הָ
b) אֵת
c) לְ
d) כָּל

2. How is the definite article pronounced in Hebrew?

a) "ha"
b) "hi"
c) "ho"
d) "hu"

3. Which of the following words does NOT use the definite article in Hebrew?

a) הַבַּיִת (the house)
b) הַסֵּפֶר (the book)
c) כְּתֻבַת (a letter)
d) הַפֶּסַח (the Passover)

4. In Hebrew, when is the definite article placed?

a) At the end of the word
b) It's a separate word of its own
c) Before the noun
d) It depends on the noun's gender and number

Chapter 5
The Noun

In Hebrew, the Verb usually comes before the Noun which is its Subject, for example, "Jonah made" is עָשָׂה יוֹנָה. The accusative case, which is the Objective in the Hebrew sentence, is frequently indicated in Hebrew by אֶת. As a result, if we want to say "Jehovah made the sea" in Hebrew, for example, it's עָשָׂה יְהוָֹה אֶת-הַיָּם.

There are relatively few nouns in Hebrew that are properly speaking primitive. The majority of them are derived from verbs, like מֶלֶךְ king, מַלְכָּה queen, מַלְכוּת and מַמְלָכָה kingdom, from the verb מָלַךְ "to rule"; אֹכֶל food from the verb אָכַל "to eat".

It's also worth mentioning that in a few instances, the process might be reversed, and verbs are derived from nouns, for example: אָהַל "to reside in a tent" is derived from the noun אֹהֶל "a tent", also, הֶאֱזִין "to hear" is derived from the noun אֹזֶן "an ear".

There are three methods in which nouns can be derived from verbs:

1. By simply altering the verb's vowel points; for example: עֶבֶד a servant, from עָבַד to work; דָּבָר a word, from דִּבֵּר to speak; חַטָּא a sinner, from חָטָא to sin.
2. By prefixing to the beginning, inserting the middle of words, or suffixing at the end, one or more of the following letters א ה ו י מ נ ת—which are called the Heemantiv letters, from the memorial word הֶאֱמַנְתִּיו— by which a great variety of forms are produced; for example: תַּכְלִית completion, from כָּלָה to finish; מַאֲכָל food, and מַאֲכֶלֶת slaughtering knife, from אָכַל to eat.
3. By eliminating one of the radicals; for example: נֵץ a flower, נָצַץ to bloom; מַד a measure, מָדַד to measure.

Speaking of derivation, it can be noted that nouns could frequently be derived from other nouns by augmentation, substitution of vowels, or composition; for example: חֹבֵל a helmsman, from חֶבֶל a cable or rope; תַּחְתוֹן nethermost parts, from תַּחַת under; קַדְמוֹן easterly, from קֶדֶם east.

Many Hebrew names are composite nouns, with the distinguishing titles of the Most High, either אֵל or יְהוָֹה, frequently appearing in full or in part within their formation. Examples of such names are חִזְקִיָּהוּ Hezekiah, which means strength of Jehovah, a combination of חָזַק strength and יְהוָֹה Jehovah; גַּבְרִיאֵל Gabriel, meaning "man of God," from the combination of גֶּבֶר a man, and אֵל God; and אֲרִיאֵל lion of God, from the combination of אֲרִי a lion, and אֵל which means God.

Gender

In English, a noun can be classified as masculine, feminine, or neuter. As a result, the noun "man" is a masculine, "woman" is feminine, and "sea" is neuter. The situation is different in Hebrew, as we only have two genders in Hebrew: masculine and feminine nouns. Just like English, male entities have masculine names, while female entities have feminine names. Hence, "a man" is denoted by אִישׁ which is a masculine noun, while a woman" is denoted by אִשָּׁה which is a feminine noun. Neuter nouns in English have entirely masculine or feminine equivalents in Hebrew. Thus, "a desert" מִדְבָּר is masculine, and "dry land" יַבָּשָׁה is feminine. However, words which in most of the

Western languages would be of the neuter gender are in Hebrew generally of the feminine.

In Hebrew, sometimes a word's form indicates its gender, and other times its meaning does.

1. Form: The majority of nouns which end in one of the original radical letters of the word are masculine; for example: קֶבֶר grave, from קָבַר to bury; דָּבָר a word, from דִּבֵּר to speak. Additionally, those ending in the letter ה preceded by Segol; for example, מוֹרֶה male teacher, שָׂדֶה field; also, those which end ending in ם ,י, or ן; for example: עִבְרִי a Hebrew, פִּדְיוֹם redemption, and קָרְבָּן an offering.
   Conversely, feminine nouns are those that end in ה, ת, ת, ית, ות; for example: דַּעַת knowledge, מוֹרָה female teacher.
2. Meaning: All nouns denoting the names and offices of men, people, rivers, mountains, months, and so on belong to the masculine nouns. All names, offices, relations of women, countries, towns, body parts are considered to be Feminine.

Common Gender nouns are those that are used in both genders, which are a considerable number of the vocabulary. The majority of birds, flocks, metals, and so on fall into this category, however they are often considered to be masculine.

There are two forms of the adjective: one for the masculine and one for the feminine. The masculine form of the adjective is used to qualify a noun that is masculine; whereas, the feminine form of the adjective is used to qualify a noun that is feminine.

The Feminine gender of nouns is formed by adding ה, ת, ת to the masculine form; for example, מוֹרֶה which is a male teacher, מוֹרָה which is a female teacher; עִבְרִי which is a Hebrew man, עִבְרִית which is a Hebrew woman. Following a guttural, the form ת appears as ת instead, for example מוֹדַעַת which means knowledge, instead of מוֹדַע.

Pluralization

Similar to the Greek Language, Hebrew too contains three number forms, which means a noun is classified as singular, dual, or plural. As a result, "boy" is singular, while "boys" is plural. When a noun refers to one item or person, it is singular; when it refers to several items or people, it is plural. The dual denotes pairs of objects, such as "two eyes", for example.

Formation of the Plural Masculine:

As far as the letters are concerned, the plural of masculine nouns is often constructed by adding the suffixing ים to the singular, for example: סוּס one horse, סוּסִים horses; מֶלֶךְ one king, מְלָכִים kings. Nevertheless, nouns ending in י take only the letter ם to be in the plural form, for example: צִי ship, צִים ships; יְהוּדִי Jew, יְהוּדִים Jews. This is done to avoid an extra Yod to be added to the singular form in order to turn it plural, which is in fact due in each of the aforementioned situations.

In some cases, one encounters certain irregular plural forms, such as מְלָכִין kings, for מְלָכִים; חַלּוֹנֵי windows, for חַלּוֹנִים.

Formation of the Plural Feminine:

The Plural of the feminine is formed either:

1. By changing the feminine singular suffixing ה, ֶת, ַת into וֹת, along with the corresponding vowel changes; for example, תּוֹרָה law, תּוֹרוֹת; טַבַּעַת a ring, טַבָּעוֹת. Though, in some cases, the word could retain the maintain the ת, for example: like דֶּלֶת a door, דְּלָתוֹת; קֶשֶׁת a bow, קְשָׁתוֹת.
2. By simply appending וֹת to the singular; for example: אוֹת a letter, אוֹתוֹת; חֶרֶב sword, חֲרָבוֹת.
3. By changing ִית into ִיּוֹת and וּת into ֻיּוֹת , for example: עִבְרִית a Hebrew woman, עִבְרִיּוֹת; מַלְכוּת kingdom, מַלְכֻיּוֹת.

Irregularities: Several masculine nouns take וֹת for the plural; for example, אָב father, אָבוֹת; צָבָא army, צְבָאוֹת; קוֹל sound, קוֹלוֹת. The opposite is often done with feminine words that take ִים in the plural form, for example: אֶבֶן stone.

Certain words indiscriminately take a masculine or feminine plural, for example: דּוֹר generation, דּוֹרִים and דּוֹרוֹת; חַלּוֹן window, חַלּוֹנִים and חַלּוֹנוֹת.

Some nouns are only found in the single form, such as metals, liquids, seasons, etc. For example: זָהָב gold, כֶּסֶף silver, יַיִן wine, שֶׁמֶן oil, אָבִיב spring, חֹרֶף winter, חוֹל sand, אָבָק dust. Meanwhile, others are found only in the plural; חַיִּים life, רַחֲמִים mercy, פָּנִים face, כְּלָיוֹת loins.

Remarks:

1. An adjective has the same gender and number as the noun it qualifies for, for example: אִישׁ טוֹב "A good man", אִשָּׁה טוֹבָה "A good woman".
2. The adjective comes after the word for which it is appropriate and the article is included in both the noun and the qualifying adjective, for example: If we wish to say "the good city", we write הָעִיר הַטּוֹבָה.
3. Because עִיר is a feminine noun, the adjective bears the feminine form.
4. Kindly note that putting the article before only the adjective, like: הָעִיר טוֹבָה would mean "The city is good," not "the good city".

Formation of the Dual:

Whether the singular is feminine or masculine, the dual is formed by appending ַיִם to the end of the word; for example: מֶלֶךְ king, מַלְכַּיִם; יוֹם day, יוֹמַיִם; אֶלֶף one thousand, אַלְפַּיִם.

When a noun ends in ָה , the ה must be replaced with ת before the dual ending is added; for example, מֵאָה one hundred, מָאתַיִם; יָרֵכָה thigh, יַרְכָּתַיִם; שָׁנָה year, שְׁנָתַיִם.

Some nouns, like the following and a few more, form their dual appending ַיִם to the plural rather than the singular; for example: חוֹמָה wall, plural would be חוֹמוֹת, the dual form would be חוֹמֹתַיִם.

The primary purpose of the dual is to designate items that are twofold in nature or in art, such as the hands יָדַיִם, the feet רַגְלַיִם, or a pair of shoes נַעֲלַיִם.

Remarks:

1. Although they are in dual form, the words מַיִם which means waters and שָׁמַיִם which means skies, are used for the plural.
2. Occasionally, the dual termination ַיִם is contracted into ֵים ; for example: שְׁנֵים which means two, for שְׁנַיִם; also, שְׁתֵּים for שְׁתַּיִם.
3. Kindly note that the vowel shifts that occur when the dual is formed are essentially the same as those that occur when the plural is formed; for example, כָּנָף wing, in the plural form כְּנָפִים, in the dual form כְּנָפַיִם.

Case

In English, there are three noun cases: the nominative, the possessive, and the objective. In Hebrew, we have three comparable instances. The Nominative is the standard form of a noun that functions as the subject of a verb. This is the standard form of the word, any change is being based on this form. The accusative could easily be recognized by the word אֶת preceding it.

We have to pay close attention to what our possessive case refers to. In English we say "the king's word", or simply "the word of the king". We modify the word "king" in one case by adding "'s," and in the other case by prefixing "of" in order to indicate the Possessive Case. Unlike the English example, the inflected word in Hebrew is "word", not "king". We have what is known as the Construct Form in a phrase like "the word of the king". The word "word" in Hebrew is the inflected word—it changes, whereas the inflected word in English is "king". We may express the distinction in this way: it would be as though we were writing the phrase in English: "the word – of the king", in Hebrew it would be: "the word of – the king".

After explaining it on English, let's see how this works in Hebrew: "the word of the king" in Hebrew is: "דְּבַר־יְהוָה". It is important to notice that while the form of the word for "the king" remains the same, the Hebrew term for "word" has changed. "The word" is הַדָּבָר in Hebrew. However, "the word of -" is represented by דְּבַר, which is called: The Construct State.

Since the words in this combination seem to have been put together solely to present a single, definite idea, the entire combination might be viewed as displaying a single compound notion. As a result, in addition to the consonant letters often changing, the word's vowels are either contracted or rejected in accordance with the standard rules governing vowel changes. The following are the most significant of these changes:

a) In the nouns with long changeable vowels in their penultimate and ultimate syllables, the vowels in the penultimate syllable fall away, and the long vowels in the ultimate syllable are changed to the equivalent short; an example of this would be: לְבַב דָּוִד heart of David, from לֵבָב. Thus, in monosyllables, יַד יְהוָה hand of Jehovah, from יָד.
b) The termination of feminine nouns ending in ָה is changed to ַת , for example, תּוֹרָה a law, תּוֹרַת מֹשֶׁה law of Moses; שִׁירָה a song, שִׁירַת דּוֹדִי a song of my beloved.
c) Masculine nouns ending in ֶה keep the ה but replace the Segol with Tseri, for example: מִקְנֶה the cattle, מִקְנֵה אַבְרָהָם the cattle of Abraham; מַחֲנֶה a camp, מַחֲנֵה יִשְׂרָאֵל camp of Israel. However, as an exception, the construct state for the word פֶּה mouth, is פִּה.
d) The ending ִים in the plural words and the ending ַיִם in the dual words are changed in the construct state to be ֵי . Meanwhile the preceding vowel or vowels, if changeable, disappear; for example: סוּסִים horses, סוּסֵי שְׁלֹמֹה horses of Solomon; דְּבָרִים words, דִּבְרֵי אֱמֶת words of truth; יָדַיִם hands, יְדֵי חַיִל⊠ hands of strength.
e) Plurals ending with וֹת experience no terminational change in the construct state; for example: בְּרָכוֹת which means blessings, בִּרְכוֹת שָׁמַיִם blessings of heaven; אָבוֹת fathers, אֲבוֹת יִשְׂרָאֵל fathers of Israel. However, you'll see that the vowels in the penultimate syllables either vanish or alter in accordance with analogy.
f) Segolate nouns[6] in the singular, excluding those that have ו or י for their middle radical, are not subject to any variation; for example, מֶלֶךְ king, מֶלֶךְ סְדֹם king of Sodom; however, בַּיִת house, בֵּית תְּפִלָּה house of prayer; מָוֶת death, should be מוֹת, where ָוֶ is contracted into וֹ: In light of this, there are a few exceptions to this rule: for example, זֶרַע, נֶטַע, קַחַת, חֶבֶל drop the first vowel in the construct state, thus, they are: זְרַע, נְטַע, קְחַת, חֲבֵל.

Remarks:

1. There are instances of doubly or even trebly constructed states sometimes; for example: תּוֹלְדוֹת בְּנֵי-נֹחַ the generations of Noah's sons; יְמֵי שְׁנֵי חַיֵּי אַבְרָהָם the days of Abraham's life.
2. Singular nouns with unchangeable vowels resist all construction related. These include things like: שִׁיר a song עִיר a city, בְּרִית a covenant, סוּס a horse, רוּחַ the wind, קוֹל a voice. These can be learned only with practice.

Exercise 5:

1. Which of the following is a characteristic of Hebrew nouns?

a) They do not have gender
b) They do not have number
c) They have gender and number
d) They have tense

[6] Segolates are words in the Hebrew language whose end is of the form CVCVC, where the penultimate vowel receives syllable stress. Such words are called "Segolates" because the final unstressed vowel is typically (but not always) Segol.

2. How many genders do Hebrew nouns have?

a) One
b) Two
c) Three
d) Four

3. In Hebrew, how is the plural form of most nouns formed?

a) By adding "ה" at the end
b) By adding "י" at the end
c) By adding " ים " at the end
d) By adding " ת " at the end

4. Which of the following is an example of a masculine noun in Hebrew?

a) מוֹדַעַת (knowledge)
b) בַּת (girl)
c) סוּס (horse)
d) בֵּיצָה (egg)

5. The feminine form of the Hebrew adjective "גָדוֹל" (big) is "...............".

6. The plural form of the Hebrew noun "סֵפֶר" (book) is "...............".

7. In Hebrew, the noun "אִישׁ" (man) is singular, and its plural form is "...............".

8. The Hebrew word "עִיר" (city) is feminine singular, and its plural form is "...............".

9. The Hebrew word "בַּיִת" (house) is singular, and its plural form is "...............".

Chapter 6
The Adjective

Hebrew adjectives are varied by gender and number just like nouns, to which they conform also in the rules of their vowel changes; for example, גָּדוֹל great (singular masculine), גְּדוֹלִים plural masculine, גְּדוֹלָה (singular feminine), גְּדוֹלוֹת (plural feminine). Additionally, they follow the analogy of nouns moreover in the mode of forming the construct state and of annexing suffixes.

Adjectives function as qualifying words and are often positioned after the corresponding nouns, as in the case of אִישׁ טוֹב a good man. However, the adjective might occasionally precede the noun, for example: גָּדוֹל עֲוֹנִי great is my sin.

The adjective also obtains the definite article when the noun is followed by the article or any of the pronominal suffixes, for example: הָאִישׁ הַטּוֹב "the good man" and הָאִשָּׁה הַטּוֹבָה "the good woman", בְּנִי הַקָּטָן "my little son", בָּנָיו הַקְּטַנִּים "his little sons". If not, the adjective stops being the qualifying word, and turns into the predicate of the substantive, for example: הָאִישׁ טוֹב "the man (is) good", בְּנִי קָטָן "my son (is) little", and so on.

When adjectives ending in Hireq and Yod, they often refer to gentile denominations, for example, עִבְרִי a Hebrew man, עִבְרִיָּה a Hebrew woman, מִצְרִי an Egyptian, יִשְׂרְאֵלִי an Israeli; except for אַכְזָרִי which means cruel, the Yod being merely paragogic.

Comparison of Adjectives

In Hebrew, the degrees of comparison are conveyed by specific accompanying words, often prepositions and adverbs, put before the adjective, rather than by a change in the adjective's form as in Latin and Greek. Thus, the preposition "מ", from "מִן", signifies "from", "than", or "in comparison of", is used to express the comparative degree when it comes to the comparison of two or more nouns and it is placed after the adjective and before the noun being compared. For example, מָתוֹק מִדְּבַשׁ "sweeter from honey" or "sweeter than honey"; טוֹב מֵחַיִּים "better than life", גָּדוֹל מִכָּל־בְּנֵי קֶדֶם "greater than all the sons of the East". Here's an example of which the comparison is constructed with a verb, מִזְּקֵנִים אֶתְבּוֹנָן "I understand more than the elders".

Occasionally, the letter מ can lend a phrase the power of a superlative, as in the case of עָרוּם מִכֹּל חַיַּת הַשָּׂדֶה "cunning above all the creatures of the field", or "the most cunning".

The Superlative degree is not denoted by a specific sign; instead, it is conveyed through a variety of circumlocutions. For example:

a) By using the intensive adverb מְאֹד very, or מְאֹד מְאֹד very, very.
b) By repeating a word in the Genitive, for example: קֹדֶשׁ הַקֳּדָשִׁים "holy of holies", i.e. the most holy place; עֶבֶד עֲבָדִים servant of servants, etc.
c) By repeating the adjective; as רַע רַע יֹאמַר הַקּוֹנֶה bad, bad, says the buyer, i.e. very bad; עָמֹק עָמֹק deep, deep, i.e. extremely deep, etc.
d) By adding the name of God to a substantive, עִיר גְּדוֹלָה לֵאלֹהִים a big city to God, i.e. very great; נְשִׂיא אֱלֹהִים a prince of God, i.e. a notably great and distinguished prince.

e) By the article prefixed to the positive, for example: בְּנוֹ הַקָּטָן his little sone or his youngest son; בְּנֵי יִשַׁי הַגְּדוֹלִים the great sons of Jesse or the eldest sons; אָחִיו הַגָּדוֹל his great brother or his eldest brother, etc.

f) By using the preposition ב "in", "among"; for example: קָטָן נְתַתִּיךָ בַּגּוֹיִם I will make you small among the nations or I will make you least; לַיִשׁ גִּבֹּר בַּבְּהֵמָה the lion strong among the beasts or the lion is the strongest, etc.

Numerals

Numerals are divided into Cardinals and Ordinals. The Cardinal numbers from one to twenty admit of gender, for example: אִישׁ אֶחָד one man; אִשָּׁה אַחַת one woman etc. Also, the numbers from one to six are f the construct state, for example: שְׁנֵי עֵדִים two (of) witnesses; שֵׁשֶׁת יָמִים six (of) days, etc.

Cardinal Numbers:

Number	Masculine Absolute	Masculine Construct	Feminine Absolute	Feminine Construct
One	אֶחָד	אַחַד	אַחַת	אַחַת
Two	שְׁנַיִם	שְׁנֵי or שְׁנַיִם	שְׁתַּיִם	שְׁתֵּי or שְׁתַּיִם
Three	שְׁלֹשָׁה	שְׁלֹשֶׁת	שָׁלֹשׁ	שְׁלֹשׁ
Four	אַרְבָּעָה	אַרְבַּעַת	אַרְבַּע	-
Five	חֲמִשָּׁה	חֲמֵשֶׁת	חָמֵשׁ	חֲמֵשׁ
Six	שִׁשָּׁה	שֵׁשֶׁת	שֵׁשׁ	שֵׁשׁ
Seven	שִׁבְעָה	שִׁבְעַת	שֶׁבַע	שְׁבַע
Eight	שְׁמוֹנָה	שְׁמוֹנַת	שְׁמֹנֶה	-
Nine	תִּשְׁעָה	תִּשְׁעַת	תֵּשַׁע	תְּשַׁע
Ten	עֲשָׂרָה	עֲשֶׂרֶת	עֶשֶׂר	-

Remarks:

1. It is noteworthy that the Cardinals from 3 to 10 belong to the feminine gender, the derivatives (ending in ָה and ַת) belong to the masculine gender, seemingly inverting the order of nature.
2. The feminine number אַחַת is a contraction for אַחֶרֶת.
3. It appears that שְׁנַיִם is the dual of the obsolete שֵׁן; Similarly, שְׁתַּיִם (for שְׁנָתַיִם) is likewise the dual of שָׁנָה, with the Dagesh serving as a compensation for the omitted נ.
4. In Genesis 27:44–Exodus 18–21, the plurals אֲחָדִים and עֲשָׂרוֹת also occur.

5. There are also several Cardinals that have suffixes attached to them, such as: שְׁנֵינוּ both of us, שְׁלָשְׁתְּכֶם you three, or the triad of you.

The intermediate numbers ranging from ten to twenty, twenty to thirty, and so forth are formed by joining a decimal and a unit in the following way:

Number	Masculine	Feminine
Eleven	אַחַת עָשָׂר	אַחַת עֶשְׂרֵה
Twelve	שְׁנֵים עָשָׂר or שְׁנֵי עָשָׂר	שְׁתֵּים עֶשְׂרֵה or שְׁתֵּי עָשְׂרֵה
Thirteen	שְׁלֹשָׁה עָשָׂר	שְׁלֹשׁ עֶשְׂרֵה
Fourteen	אַרְבָּעָה עָשָׂר	אַרְבַּע עֶשְׂרֵה
Twenty one	אֶחָד וְעֶשְׂרִים	אַחַת וְעֶשְׂרִים
Twenty two	שְׁנַיִם וְעֶשְׂרִים	שְׁתַּיִם וְעֶשְׂרִים

The decimals ranging from thirty to ninety are represented by the plural forms of the corresponding units; for example, שְׁלֹשִׁים thirty, אַרְבָּעִים forty, חֲמִשִּׁים fifty, and so forth; apart from עֶשְׂרִים twenty, which is the plural of עֶשֶׂר ten.

Hundreds and Thousands:

Hundreds and thousands are represented as the plural forms of the words מֵאָה hundred and אֶלֶף thousand," preceded by the nine units, as follows:

One hundred	מֵאָה
Two hundred	מָאתַיִם
Three hundred	שְׁלֹשׁ מֵאוֹת
Four hundred	אַרְבַּע מֵאוֹת
Three thousand	שְׁלֹשֶׁת אֲלָפִים
Four thousand	אַרְבַּעַת אֲלָפִים
A hundred thousand	מְאַת or מֵאָה אֶלֶף
Six hundred thousand	שֵׁשׁ מֵאוֹת אֶלֶף

Ordinal Numbers:

The following table shows how the Ordinal numbers, which are —aside from רִאשׁוֹן the first—are obtained from the Cardinals by adding the terminations ִי and ִית . Nonetheless, the majority of them insert ִי also before the ground form's last letter.

Number	Masculine	Feminine
First	רִאשׁוֹן	רִאשֹׁנָה
Second	שֵׁנִי	שֵׁנִית
Third	שְׁלִישִׁי	שְׁלִישִׁית
Fourth	רְבִיעִי	רְבִיעִית
Fifth	חֲמִישִׁי	חֲמִישִׁית
Sixth	שִׁשִּׁי	שִׁשִּׁית
Seventh	שְׁבִיעִי	שְׁבִיעִית
Eighth	שְׁמִינִי	שְׁמִינִית
Ninth	תְּשִׁיעִי	תְּשִׁיעִית
Tenth	עֲשִׂירִי	עֲשִׂירִית

Since the ordinal numbers only go up to ten, the Hebrews used the Cardinals to indicate the ordinals when the enumeration went beyond this. But then the number always followed the noun, or the noun was repeated, for example: שְׁנֵים עָשָׂר יוֹם Twelve days (cardinal), and הַיּוֹם הַשְּׁנֵים עָשָׂר the twelfth day; שְׁנַת הַחֲמִשִּׁים or שְׁנַת הַחֲמִשִּׁים שָׁנָה the fiftieth year. Thus, below ten בִּשְׁנַת אַרְבַּע in the fourth year; יוֹם אֶחָד the first day.

Fractional Numbers:

These are חֵצִי (masculine), מֶחֱצָה (feminine) a half, (masculine construct חֲצִי, feminine מַחְצַת or מַחֲצִית). The remaining fractional numbers are expressed by putting the feminine ordinals before the noun; for example, שְׁלִישִׁית הַשָּׁנָה the third (part) of a year; whereas שָׁנָה הַשְּׁלִישִׁית means the third year. Sometimes the noun is omitted, like in Genesis 47:24, where it says, "And ye shall give חֲמִישִׁית "a fifth" unto Pharaoh".

Notation Technique:

The Hebrews employed the alphabet's letters to represent numerals. For this reason, they divided the letters—including the last ones—into three groups, the first of which stood for units, the second for tens, and the third for hundreds;

Units	1	2	3	4	5	6	7	8	9
	א	ב	ג	ד	ה	ו	ז	ח	ט
Tens	10	20	30	40	50	60	70	80	90
	י	כ	ל	מ	נ	ס	ע	פ	צ

Hundreds	100	200	300	400	500	600	700	800	900
	ק	ר	ש	ת	ך	ם	ן	ף	ץ

Beyond ten they joined a decimal and a unit as follows:

11	12	13	21	22	31	32	41	42
י׳א	י׳ב	י׳ג	כ׳א	כ׳ב	ל׳א	ל׳ב	מ׳א	מ׳ב

They always used ט׳ו for fifteen, 15=6×9=ט׳ו, instead of י׳ה, as the latter is a contraction of the term יְהֹוָה Jehovah. When reaching the hundred, numbers were formed in the same way, for example: 103 ק׳ג ,102 ק׳ב ,101 ק׳א, etc. They started the alphabet again and added two dots to each letter to represent thousands and greater numbers, thus: 1834 אֽ̈תּל׳ד ,3000 ג̈ ,2000 ב̈ ,1000 א̈, etc.

Although this method of enumeration is absent from the Hebrew Bible, which always expresses numbers in words, it is noteworthy that it was used by the Masorites and was also used by Buxtorf in the citation of chapters and verses in his excellent Hebrew Concordance.

Exercise 6:

1. What are the two main types of numerals?

  a) Cardinal and Ordinal
  b) Prime and Composite
  c) Roman and Arabic
  d) Binary and Decimal

2. Which gender does the definite adjective agree with in Hebrew?

  a) Masculine
  b) Feminine
  c) Neuter
  d) Both A and B

3. Which numeral represents the number "five" in Hebrew?

  a) שְׁנַיִם (Shnayim)
  b) שְׁלֹשָׁה (Shlosha)
  c) חֲמִשָּׁה (Chamisha)
  d) שִׁשָּׁה (Shisha)

4. What is the Hebrew word for "hundred"?

a) מֵאָה (Meah)
b) עֶשְׂרִים (Eserim)
c) חֲמִשָּׁה-עָשָׂר (Chamisha-Asar)
d) מָאתַיִם (Matayim)

5. Which Hebrew letter has the numerical value of 10?

a) י
b) ח
c) ק
d) ס

6. The ordinal number for "five" in Hebrew is "............... (masculine)" and "............... (feminine)".

7. The Hebrew word for "seven" is "............... (masculine)" and "............... (feminine)".

8. The Hebrew number "ten" is written as "............... (masculine)" and "............... (feminine)".

9. In Hebrew, "eleven" is written as "............... (masculine)" and "............... (feminine)".

10. The Hebrew word for "fifty" is "...............".

11. The ordinal number for "nine" in Hebrew is "............... (masculine)" and "............... (feminine)".

12. The Hebrew word for "three" is "............... (masculine)" and "............... (feminine)".

13. "Sixty four" in Hebrew is written as "...............".

14. The Hebrew numeral for "one hundred" is "...............".

15. The comparative form of "good" in Hebrew is "...............".

16. The superlative form of "beautiful" in Hebrew is "...............".

17. The comparative form of "happy" in Hebrew is "...............".

Bottom of Form

Chapter 7
The Pronoun

Like in most other languages, Hebrew pronouns can be classified as Personal, Demonstrative, Relative, or Interrogative.

What are occasionally called in other languages: Possessive Pronouns, do not exist in Hebrew as independent words. In Hebrew, certain pronominal appendages attached to the end of nouns show the relation of possession; a detailed explanation will be further provided.

Personal Pronouns

The Hebrew Personal Pronoun has two forms: one that is separable and the other that is inseparable. The first is used in the following situations, where a pronoun of any person is employed as the nominative to a verb, and it is as follows:

Singular			**Plural**		
Masculine & Feminine	אֲנִי, אנֹכִי	I	Masculine & Feminine	אֲנוּ, נַחְנוּ, אֲנַחְנוּ	We
Masculine	אַתָּה	You	Masculine	אַתֶּם	You
Feminine	אַתְּ	You	Feminine	אַתֶּן	You
Masculine	הוּא	He	Masculine	הֵם	They
Feminine	הִיא	She	Feminine	הֵן	They

On the other hand, the inseparable personal pronouns are fragments of the separable ones, and are always affixed, or formally prefixed or suffixed, to the beginning or end of other speech parts, such as nouns, verbs, adverbs, or prepositions. Thus, אָבִי my father, from אָב father and ִי which is a fragment of אֲנִי I; דְּבָרוֹ his word from דָּבָר and a fragment of הוּא he.

Similarly, the verb persons and tenses are indicated; pronoun fragments in the past tense are postfixed, while in the future, they are postfixed and prefixed. Therefore, by appending תָּ (from אַתָּה you) to the root קָטַל he killed, we have קָטַלְתָּ you killed; and by appending נוּ (from אֲנַחְנוּ we) we have קָטַלְנוּ we killed; also, by appending אֶ (from אֲנִי I) to קְטֹל, we have the future אֶקְטֹל I will kill; תִּ (from אַתָּה you) it gives us תִּקְטֹל you will kill, etc.

Moreover, the objective pronouns are likewise indicated by subjoining other fragments to either of these tenses; for example, אֶקְטְלֵהוּ I will kill him; קְטַלְתִּיהוּ I killed him; קְטַלְתִּיךָ I killed you; וְיִקְטְלֵנִי and he will kill me.

Similarly, the prepositions מִ, לְ, בְ, etc. are used with the inseparable pronouns that describe relations equivalent to cases in other languages; for example: לִי to me, אוֹתִי me, בִּי in me, etc.

Thus, the inseparable suffix pronouns provide the position of possessives, as remarked above.

The different suffixes and how they are appended to nouns of both genders are shown in the following table, along with the changes they make to these nouns' forms.

דָבָר, a word, Masculine							
Singular				**Plural**			
Masculine & Feminine	ִי	דְבָרִי	My word	Masculine & Feminine	ַי	דְבָרַי	My words
Masculine	ְךָ	דְבַרְךָ	Your word	Masculine	ֶיךָ	דְבָרֶיךָ	Your words
Feminine	ֵךְ	דְבָרֵךְ	Your word	Feminine	ַיִךְ	דְבָרַיִךְ	Your words
Masculine	וֹ	דְבָרוֹ	His word	Masculine	ָיו	דְבָרָיו	His words
Feminine	ָהּ	דְבָרָהּ	Her word	Feminine	ֶיהָ	דְבָרֶיהָ	Her words
Masculine & Feminine	ֵנוּ	דְבָרֵנוּ	Our word	Masculine & Feminine	ֵינוּ	דִבְרֵינוּ	Our words
Masculine	ְכֶם	דְבַרְכֶם	Your word	Masculine	ֵיכֶם	דִבְרֵיכֶם	Your words
Feminine	ְכֶן	דְבַרְכֶן	Your word	Feminine	ֵיכֶן	דִבְרֵיכֶן	Your words
Masculine	ָם	דְבָרָם	Their word	Masculine	ֵיהֶם	דִבְרֵיהֶם	Their words
Feminine	ָן	דְבָרָן	Their word	Feminine	ֵיהֶן	דִבְרֵיהֶן	Their words

שָׁנָה, a year, Feminine							
Singular				**Plural**			
Masculine & Feminine	ִי	שְׁנָתִי	My year	Masculine & Feminine	ַי	שְׁנוֹתַי	My years
Masculine	ְךָ	שְׁנָתְךָ	Your year	Masculine	ֶיךָ	שְׁנוֹתֶיךָ	Your years
Feminine	ֵךְ	שְׁנָתֵךְ	Your year	Feminine	ַיִךְ	שְׁנוֹתַיִךְ	Your years
Masculine	וֹ	שְׁנָתוֹ	His year	Masculine	ָיו	שְׁנוֹתָיו	His years
Feminine	ָהּ	שְׁנָתָהּ	Her year	Feminine	ֶיהָ	שְׁנוֹתֶיהָ	Her years

Masculine & Feminine	ֵנוּ	שְׁנָתֵנוּ	Our year	Masculine & Feminine	ֵינוּ	שְׁנוֹתֵינוּ	Our years
Masculine	כֶם	שְׁנַתְכֶם	Your year	Masculine	ֵיכֶם	שְׁנוֹתֵיכֶם	Your years
Feminine	כֶן	שְׁנַתְכֶן	Your year	Feminine	ֵיכֶן	שְׁנוֹתֵיכֶן	Your years
Masculine	ָם	שְׁנָתָם	Their year	Masculine	ֵיהֶם	שְׁנוֹתֵיהֶם	Their years
Feminine	ָן	שְׁנָתָן	Their year	Feminine	ֵיהֶן	שְׁנוֹתֵיהֶן	Their years

The vowel indicated as pertaining to the letter that comes directly before the suffix is termed the union-vowel. Thus, the Tseri in דְּבָרֵךְ and the Segol in שְׁנוֹתֶיךָ are union-vowels.

Vowel and Literal Changes as a Result of Suffixes:

a) When a noun ends in a vowel, it takes on the suffix without a union-vowel; for example, אָבִי father, אָבִיהָ her father, אֲבִיהֶם their father. When a noun ends in a consonant, the situation is different; for example, סוּס horse, סוּסָה her horse, where the Kamets is the union-vowel.

b) The feminine nouns ending in ָה before the ordinary suffix is altered to ַת ; but, it is altered to ַת before the grave suffixes כֶם and כֶן; for example: סוּסָה, which means a female horse, will be סוּסָתִי and סוּסַתְכֶם.

c) Nouns ending in ֶה drop the ֶה before suffixes; for example: מוֹרֶה teacher, will be מוֹרִי my teacher.

d) Characteristic termination in the plural nouns ִים is dropped before the suffix; for example: דְּבָרֵנוּ our words, not דְּבָרִימֵנוּ.

e) In the Segolates of the form מָוֶת death, the vowels are contracted before the suffixes into Cholam, as in תּוֹכְכֶם the midst of you, from תָּוֶךְ. However, for the form of בַּיִת house, the contraction is in Tseri; for example: זֵיתוֹ his olive.

f) Tseri of the ultimate before ךְ is changed into Segol or Chireq; for example: שׁוֹמֵר will be שׁוֹמֶרְךָ; אוֹיֵב will be אוֹיִבְךָ.

g) The penultimate's Cholam is replaced with Kamets Chateph or Kibbuts; for example: קֹדֶשׁ will be קָדְשׁוֹ, קֹמֶץ will be קָמְצֵיכֶם.

Demonstrative Pronouns

The Hebrew has just the following Demonstrative Pronouns:

Singular			Plural		
Masculine	זֶה	This	Masculine & Feminine	אֵלֶּה	These
Feminine	זוֹ, זאת	This			

The third-person personal pronouns הֵן , הִיא,הֵם, הוּא are often used as demonstratives. In such situation, they usually have the article prefixed; for example: הַיּוֹם הַהוּא this day.

The Relative Pronoun

There is just one relative pronoun recognized in Hebrew, אֲשֶׁר which means who, which, what and is the same for every gender and number.

This pronoun is often used before other words in its shortened form, which is שָׁ ,שַׁ ,שֶׁ, with the first and last letters being omitted. Thus, שַׁקַּמְתִּי for אֲשֶׁר קַמְתִּי until I arose; שֶׁאַתָּה for אֲשֶׁר אַתָּה which you; שֶׁעָלוּ for אֲשֶׁר עָלוּ they who went up.

Even though it is a relative pronoun, אֲשֶׁר is frequently used as a conjunction. For example, in the sentence "Because he informed him that he was a Jew - אֲשֶׁר יְהוּדִי.

In certain cases, the demonstratives זוּ ,זֶה can fulfil the role of a relative pronoun; for example: עַם זֶה קָנִיתָ the people you have purchased; for אֲשֶׁר קָנִיתָ.

Interrogative Pronouns

There are two Interrogative Pronouns: מִי who, and מָה מַה) and מֶה) what; Whereas the former applied to persons and the latter applied to objects; for example, מִי אַתָּה who are you? מָה אֹמַר How shall I say? מַה־טּוֹב How wonderful! מַה־נּוֹרָא How horrible!

The form מֶה is commonly used before the Gutturals א ,ה ,ח ,ע whenever they have Kamets; for example: מֶה אָנֹכִי who am I? In the absence of Kamets, מַה usually comes before these letters.

Exercise 7:

1. What is the Hebrew word for the pronoun "I"?

a) אתה (Ata)
b) אני (Ani)

c) הוא (Hu)
d) היא (Hi)

2. Which pronoun is used to refer to a group of people in Hebrew?

a) אתה (Ata)
b) היא (Hi)
c) אני (Ani)
d) אנחנו (Anachnu)

3. What is the Hebrew word for "you" (singular, masculine)?

(a אתה (Ata)
b) את (At)
c) היא (Hi)
d) הוא (Hu)

4. Which pronoun is used to refer to a female in Hebrew?

a) הוא (Hu)
b) היא (Hi)
c) אתה (Ata)
d) אני (Ani)

5. Which pronoun is used to refer to an object or thing in Hebrew?

a) היא (Hi)
b) הוא (Hu)
c) זה (Ze)
d) אני (Ani)

6. Which pronoun is used to refer to a group of females in Hebrew?

a) הן (Hen)
b) הם (Hem)
c) אתן (Aten)
d) אני (Ani)

7. The plural form of "you" (masculine) in Hebrew is "...............".

8. The first person singular pronoun in Hebrew is "...............".

9. The feminine plural form of "they" in Hebrew is "...............".

10. The Hebrew word for "we" (feminine) is "...............".

11. The Hebrew word for "they" (masculine) is "...............".

12. The feminine singular form of "you" in Hebrew is "...............".

Chapter 8
The Preposition

Prepositions of בְּ ,כְּ ,לְ and מִ, מֵ

Of the prepositions, the four that follow— בְּ in, כְּ as, לְ to, מִ or מֵ from —are particularly significant due to the fact that they are united with the words that they control, such as בְּדָבָר in a word, כְּדָבָר as a word, לְדָבָר to a word, מִדָּבָר from a word, and due to their being subject to a variety of vowel pointing.

They use simple Sheva as their proper punctuation, but:

a) Before the composite Shevas, they take the corresponding short vowel; for example: כַּאֲרִי as a lion, בֶּאֱמֶת in truth.
b) Before simple Sheva they take short Chireq; for example: לִבְנֵי, בִּדְבַר.
c) When the article is omitted before nouns, they assume its punctuation, as לַמֶּלֶךְ for לְהַמֶּלֶךְ to the king, בָּעָם for בְּהָעָם among the people, בֶּהָרִים for בְּהֶהָרִים in the mountains.

There are also some other important prepositions, some of them are:

1. אֶל - "To" or "Towards": The preposition "אֶל" signifies direction or destination, indicating movement towards a specific target. For example: הָלַךְ אֶל הַחֲנוּת, which means: "He went to the store".

2. עַל - "On" or "Upon": The preposition "עַל" denotes location or position above a surface or object. For example: הַסֵּפֶר נִמְצָא עַל הַשֻּׁלְחָן, which means: "The book is on the table".

3. עִם - "With": The preposition "עִם" signifies accompaniment or association, indicating the presence of another entity. For example: אֲנִי הוֹלֵךְ עִם חֲבֵרִי, which means: "I am going with my friend".

4. לְמַעַן - "For the sake of" or "In order to": The preposition "לְמַעַן" expresses purpose or intention behind an action. For example: הוּא עוֹשֶׂה זֹאת לְמַעַן הַשָּׁלוֹם, which means: "He does it for the sake of peace".

5. עַד - "Until" or "Up to": The preposition "עַד" denotes a limit or endpoint in time, space, or quantity. For example: אֲנִי אֶצְטָרֵךְ עַד הַחֲמִשָּׁה, which means: "I will need it until five o'clock".

6. מִתּוֹךְ (Mitokh) - "From within" or "Out of": The preposition "מִתּוֹךְ" indicates the origin or source from which something emerges or originates. For example: הַיְּהוּדִים יָצְאוּ מִתּוֹךְ מִצְרַיִם, which means: "The Jews came out of Egypt".

These prepositions are united with suffixes as in the following table:

בְּ in			**לְ to**		
Singular			Singular		
Masculine & Feminine	בִּי	In me	Masculine & Feminine	לִי	To me
Masculine	בְּךָ	In you	Masculine	לְךָ	To you
Feminine	בָּךְ	In you	Feminine	לָךְ	To you
Masculine	בּוֹ	In him	Masculine	לוֹ	To him
Feminine	בָּהּ	In her	Feminine	לָהּ	To her
Plural			Plural		
Masculine & Feminine	בָּנוּ	In us	Masculine & Feminine	לָנוּ	To us
Masculine	בָּכֶם	In you	Masculine	לָכֶם	To you
Feminine	בָּכֶן	In you	Feminine	לָכֶן	To you
Masculine	בָּהֶם, בָּם	In them	Masculine	לָהֶם	To them
Feminine	בָּהֶן, בָּהֵן	In them	Feminine	לָהֶן	To them

כְּ as or like			**מִן from**		
Singular			Singular		
Masculine & Feminine	כָּמוֹנִי	Like me	Masculine & Feminine	מִמֶּנִּי, מִנִּי	From me
Masculine	כָּמוֹךָ	Like you	Masculine	מִמְּךָ, מִמֵּךְ	From you
Feminine	....	....	Feminine	מִמֵּךְ	From you
Masculine	כָּמוֹהוּ	Like him	Masculine	מִמֶּנּוּ	From him
Feminine	כָּמוֹהָ	Like her	Feminine	מִמֶּנָּה	From her
Plural			Plural		
Masculine & Feminine	כָּמוֹנוּ	Like us	Masculine & Feminine	מִמֶּנּוּ	From us
Masculine	כָּכֶם, כְּמוֹכֶם	Like you	Masculine	מִכֶּם	From you
Feminine	....	....	Feminine	מִכֶּן	From you
Masculine	כָּהֶם, כְּמוֹהֶם	Like them	Masculine	מֵהֶם	From them
Feminine	....	....	Feminine	מֵהֶן	From them

Preposition of אֵת (or אֶת)

"אֶת" (Et) is a preposition commonly used to mark the either direct object or as a sign of accusative in Hebrew.

אֵת as Sign of Accusative			אֵת as Preposition		
Singular			Singular		
Masculine & Feminine	אוֹתִי, אֹתִי	me	Masculine & Feminine	אִתִּי	With me
Masculine	אֹתְךָ	you	Masculine	אִתְּךָ	With you
Feminine	אֹתָךְ	you	Feminine	אִתָּךְ	With you
Masculine	אֹתוֹ	him	Masculine	אִתּוֹ	With him
Feminine	אֹתָהּ	her	Feminine	אִתָּהּ	With her
Plural			Plural		
Masculine & Feminine	אֹתָנוּ	us	Masculine & Feminine	אִתָּנוּ	With us
Masculine	אֹתְכֶם, אֶתְכֶם	you	Masculine	אִתְּכֶם	With you
Feminine	....	....	Feminine	....	....
Masculine	אֶתְהֶם, אֹתָם	them	Masculine	אִתָּם	With them
Feminine	אֶתְהֶן, אֹתָן	them	Feminine	....	....

Exercise 8:

1. What is the Hebrew word for "in"?

   a) בְּ (Be)
   b) מִן (Min)
   c) אֶת (Et)
   d) עַל (Al)

2. Which preposition is used to indicate movement towards a location in Hebrew?

   a) מִן (Min)
   b) אֶל (El)
   c) עַל (Al)
   d) כְּ (Ke)

3. What is the Hebrew preposition for "from"?

a) מִן (Min)
b) לְ (Le)
c) עַל (Al)
d) עִם (Im)

4. The Hebrew preposition "עַל" (Al) can mean:

a) In
b) On
c) From
d) With

5. What is the Hebrew preposition for "with"?

a) לְ (Le)
b) עַל (Al)
c) אֶת (Et)
d) עִם (Im)

6. The preposition "לְ" (Le) is often used to indicate:

a) To
b) From
c) With
d) In

7. The Hebrew preposition "כְּ" (Ke) can mean:

a) With
b) Like
c) From
d) In

8. What is the Hebrew preposition for "at"?

a) מִן (Min)
b) בְּ (Be)
c) עַל (Al)
d) אֶל (El)

9. The Hebrew preposition for "to" is "...............".

10. The preposition "מִן" (Min) can mean "..............." in Hebrew.

11. The Hebrew preposition "עַל" (Al) can mean "...............".

12. The Hebrew preposition for "with" is "...............".

13. The Hebrew preposition "עִם" (Im) can mean "..............." in Hebrew.

Chapter 9
Conjunctions

1. וְ - "And": The copulative particle וְ is by far the most significant conjunction. Considering punctuation, plain Sheva is the appropriate point; for example: מֹשֶׁה וְכָלֵב Moses and Caleb. However:

a) Before Gutturals with composite Sheva, it takes the corresponding short vowel; for example: as in וֶאֱמֶת, וַעֲבֹד.
b) It usually takes Kamets before a tone-syllable, for example: in דּוֹר וָדוֹר generation after generation; וָפַחַת and a pit.
c) Before Yod which would analogically have simple Sheva, it takes long Chireq and makes the Yod quiescent; for example: וִימֵי, וִיהִי.
d) It takes Shureq usually before words that start with either פ, מ, ו, ב and always before a letter that starts with Sheva; for example: וּפַרְעֹה, וּבַיִת, וּמֶלֶךְ, וּלְכֹל.
e) It occasionally takes Chireq Qatan or Segol before the verbs הָיָה and חָיָה; for example: as in וִחְיוּ, וִחְיִיתֶם, וֶהְיֵה.

The conjunction in Hebrew is always written as prefixed to a word unless there is a good reason for not doing so.

2. כִּי - "Because" or "That": כִּי, which is pronounced similarly to the word "key," is another often used conjunction. It denotes "that", "because", "for", or "when" as it's used to introduce explanation or reason clauses in Hebrew. For example:

מַה־זֹּאת עָשִׂיתָ כִּי יָדְעוּ הָאֲנָשִׁים כִּי מִלִּפְנֵי יְהוָה הוּא בֹרֵחַ כִּי הִגִּיד לָהֶם

Here we have this conjunction three times. The first means "for," the second "that," and the third "for".

3. אוֹ - "Or": There is also the conjunction אוֹ, which means "or" and is used to present alternatives or choices between two options. It serves to connect different terms or sentences that relate to either the first possibility or the second.

4. אִם - "If": The conjunction "אִם" is used to introduce conditional clauses or express uncertainty. For example: אִם תִּרְצֶה, אֲנִי יָכוֹל לְהַגִּיעַ לְעֶזְרָתְךָ, which means: "If you want, I can come to help you".

5. אַךְ - "But" or "However": The conjunction "אַךְ" indicates contrast or contradiction, introducing an opposing idea. For example: הַקַּיִץ חַם מְאוֹד, אַךְ הַיָּם קַר, which means: "The summer is very hot, but the sea is cold".

6. גַּם - "Also" or "And": The conjunction "גַּם" is used to add additional information or emphasize similarity. For example: גַּם אֲנִי רוֹצֶה לָלֶכֶת לְקוֹלְנוֹעַ, which means: "I also want to go to the cinema".

7. אוּלָם - "However" or "Nevertheless": The conjunction "אוּלָם" introduces a contrasting idea or exception to the previous statement. For example: הוּא עָשָׂה טָעוּת, אוּלָם לָמַד מִמֶּנָּה, which means: "He made a mistake, however, he learned from it".

8. אַף עַל פִּי שֶׁ - "Although" or "Despite": The conjunction "אַף עַל פִּי שֶׁ" introduces concessive clauses, expressing contrast or unexpected outcome. For example: אַף עַל פִּי ש הוּא עָיֵף, הוּא עֲדַיִן עוֹבֵד, which means: "Although he is tired, he is still working".

9. בְּכָל זֹאת - "Nevertheless" or "However": The phrase "בְּכָל זֹאת" is used to introduce a contrasting idea or counterargument. For example: הוּא לֹא אוֹהֵב גִילוּד, בְּכָל זֹאת הוּא אוֹכֵל אֶת כָּל הַגְּלִידָה, which means: "He doesn't like ice cream, however, he eats all of it".

10. גַּם לֹא - "Nor": The phrase "גַּם לֹא" is used to indicate negation or refusal of both options. For example: הוּא לֹא רוֹצֶה לָצֵאת לְחֹפֶשׁ, גַּם לֹא לַעֲבֹד, which means: "He doesn't want to go on vacation, nor does he want to work".

Exercise 9:

1. What is the Hebrew word for "and"?

a) וְ (Ve)
b) אוֹ (O)
c) אִם (Im)
d) כִּי (Ki)

2. Which conjunction is used to express "or" in Hebrew?

a) וְ (Ve)
b) אוֹ (O)
c) אִם (Im)
d) כִּי (Ki)

3. The conjunction "כִּי" (Ki) is often translated as:

a) And
b) Or
c) That
d) But

4. Which conjunction is used to introduce a reason or explanation in Hebrew?

a) וְ (Ve)
b) אוֹ (O)
c) אִם (Im)
d) כִּי (Ki)

5. What is the Hebrew word for "but"?

a) וְ (Ve)
b) אוֹ (O)
c) אִם (Im)
d) אַךְ (Ach)

6. Which conjunction is used to introduce a conditional clause in Hebrew?

a) וְ (Ve)
b) אוֹ (O)
c) אִם (Im)
d) כִּי (Ki)

7. What is the Hebrew word for "nor"?

a) וְ (Ve)
b) אוֹ (O)
c) גַּם לֹא (Gam Lo)
d) וְגַם (VeGam)

8. The Hebrew conjunction for "and" is "..............".

9. The conjunction "אוֹ" (O) is often translated as "..............".

10. "כִּי" (Ki) is used to introduce ".............." and ".............." clauses in Hebrew.

11. The Hebrew conjunction for "because" is "..............".

12. The Hebrew conjunction "אִם" (Im) can mean "..............".

13. The conjunction "גַּם" (Gam) is often translated as "..............".

14. "אַךְ" (Ach) is used to indicate ".............." or ".............." in Hebrew.

15. The conjunction "אוּלָם" (Ulum) is often translated as "..............".

16."אַף עַל פִּי שֶׁ" (Af Al Pi She) is used to introduce ".............." in Hebrew.

Chapter 10
Hebrew Verb System

The verb is without a doubt the most significant component of speech in Hebrew grammar as it is the basis from which most of the other components are produced and because understanding it is essential to understanding all other grammar-related concepts. Similar to the noun, the verb in Hebrew is categorized into three categories:

a) Primitive: that is, verbs that have no other word or part of speech as their root; for example, מָלַךְ to reign; יָשַׁב to sit; and דָּבַר to speak.
b) Derivatives: or those created from Primitives by initial affixes or by altering the vowel points; for example, the derivative verb נִשְׁבַּר "was broken", and the derivative verb הִשְׁבִּיר "caused to break", the derivative verb שִׁבֵּר "to break violently", from the primitive שָׁבַר "to break". As a result, derivative verbs are used in all save the last conjugation, which is primitive in comparison to the others.
c) Denominatives: those are verbs produced from nouns (de nomine); for example: אָהַל to live in tents, from אֹהֶל a tent; לָבַן to make brick, from לְבֵנָה a brick; עָרַף to break the neck, from עֹרֶף the neck.

Note: This categorization is clearly subject to substantial dispute, at least with regard to the derivatives, as it places one version of the same verb in a different class of verbs than another. However, as the distinction is maintained in all notable Hebrew grammars and does not result in a significant practical mistake, we have decided to keep it.

The parts of the verb that express the main meaning are called the Root and the original verb letters are Radical letters, respectively, while the added letters made for the sake of inflection are called Serviles. Although there are a few instances of quadriliteral and even quinquiliteral roots, Hebrew roots are mostly triliteral. Verbs that maintain their original radical letters through all of their modifications are considered regular; verbs that are pluriliteral or that lose or assimilate one or more of their radical letters are considered irregular.

The Serviles consist only of the following letters: ת, ש, נ, מ, ל, כ, י, ו, ה, ב, א; they are sometimes combined to form the memorial phrase: מֹשֶׁה וְכָלֵב אֵיתָן Moses and Caleb the Strong. The Serviles got their name because they serve as prefixes, suffixes, and so forth in the many changes that verbs and nouns go through throughout formation and flexion. So, in a word like תִּתְמַצֶּאנָה, all the letters in are therefore serviles, with the exception of מ, צ, א, which are the root. On the other hand, every letter in the alphabet is included in the list of Radicals; nonetheless, the other letters—all of them save the ones listed above—are never employed in the role of Serviles, ר, ק, צ, פ, ע, ס, ט, ח, ז, ד, ג. The main goal of using the Lexicon to determine the meaning of Hebrew words is to be able to distinguish easily between the radical and servile letters—that is, to know which to keep and which to discard. This can only be attained by having a solid understanding of word structures and significant language practice.

It is common to identify a verb's radical letters as first, second, and third radicals, depending on whatever reading order they occur in. Therefore, in the verb שָׁבַר, the first radical letter is שׁ, the second radical letter is ב, and the third radical letter is ר.

A verb's radical consonants and their corresponding vowel-points make up its ground-form, which is typically the third person singular of the the verb "Kal" - will be further explained. Any modification to this form, whether through deletion or substitution of letters or points, will inevitably produce a difference of form indicative of a new modification of the sense. Thus, from ground-form שָׁבַר to break, comes שָׁבוּר broken, שָׁבַרְתִּי I have broken, שְׁבַרְתֶּם you have broken, אֶשְׁבֹּר I will break, etc.

It is usual to use the radical letters of the verb פָּעַל to act independently as a technical designation of the several letters of any triliteral root for purposes of convenience, especially in distinguishing the various classes of irregular verbs. For example, since Pe פ is the root's first letter, Ayin ע is its second, and Lamed ל is its third, the verb נוּחַ "to rest", can be classified as a verb of Pe Nun פ"נ because its first radical is נ, or Ayin Vav ע"ו because its second letter is ו, or Lamed Cheth ל"ח or Lamed Guttural because of its third letter, which is also a Guttural. However, for reasons that will become clearer later, it is seldom required for more than one radical of the same root to be characterized in this way.

The main verb classes that may be identified in this way are as follows:

a) Those that are called Pe Gutturals because they have a Guttural as their first radical; for example:
   אָמַר to say
   הָלַךְ to go
   עָמַד to stand
   חָמַד to desire
   designated as verbs Pe פ Gutturals.

b) Those whose first radical is Yod (י); for example:
   יָדַע to know
   יָלַד to give birth
   יָשַׁב to sit
   designated as verbs פ"י.

c) Those whose first radical is Nun (נ); for example:
   נָתַן to give
   נָגַשׁ to strike
   נָטַף to distil
   designated as verbs פ"נ.

d) Those whose second and third radicals are alike; for example:
   תָּמַם to be perfect
   סָבַב to surround
   designated as verbs ע"ע (Double Ayin).

e) Those whose second radical is Vav (ו); for example:
   שׁוּב to return
   קוּם to arise
   נוּר to shine
   designated as verbs ע"ו.

f) Those whose third radical is Aleph (א); for example:
מָצָא to find
מָלָא to fill
קָרָא to call
} designated as verbs ל״א.

g) Those whose third radical is He (ה); for example:
גָּלָה to reveal
קָנָה to possess
כָּלָה to finish
} designated as verbs ל״ה.

Inflection (Conjugation)

In strict propriety of speech, Hebrew verbs are conjugate-free, at least in the sense that the term is used in reference to Greek, Latin, and other languages. Nevertheless, grammarians continue to use the word in the absence of a better one to indicate the various forms that the same verb can take in order to express different shades of meaning. There are seven different conjugations or forms that go by the names Kal, Niphal, Piel, Pual, Hiphil, Hophal, and Hithpael. The meaning of four of these—Kal, Piel, Hiphil, and Hithpael—is active, but the meaning of the other three is mostly passive.

With the exception of the first, the names of these conjugations are simply derived from the various forms of the previously mentioned verb פָּעַל, which was used as a paradigm or model verb by the earlier Jewish grammarians to demonstrate the conjugations, and to refer to modes of pronouncing those forms. Thus:

1. פָּעַל – Paal, he acted.
2. נִפְעַל – Niphal, he was acted upon.
3. פִּעֵל – Piel, he acted vigorously.
4. פֻּעַל – Pual, he was vigorously acted upon.
5. הִפְעִיל – Hiphil, he caused to act.
6. הָפְעַל – Hophal, he was caused to act.
7. הִתְפַּעֵל – Hithpael, he acted upon himself.

These several forms were used as technical terminology to denote the primary branches or conjugations of the verb in general, perhaps under the belief that the substance of the verb consisted in "action" which is perfectly reflected by the verb פָּעַל. However, because the second radical (ע) is a guttural and rejects Dagesh due as a feature of several of the conjugations, it destroys the regular analogy of the form. As a result, it was later properly abandoned as a paradigm and replaced by פָּקַד by the majority of earlier Christian grammarians. However, this was also met with criticism because פּ was one of the Aspirates and did not demonstrate the verb in its most basic form, in addition to occasionally needing a Dagesh Lene. The same observation holds true for כָּתַב, which may be found in various other grammars as well as Ewald's. Maybe there isn't a more fitting verb to use for this than לָמַר to learn or קָטַל to kill, the latter of which is used in this book as well as by Gesenius and Stuart.

For the first conjugation, Kal קַל, which means light, is uniformly employed, instead of Paal, which analogy would require. This indicates that the verb occurs in its most basic and simplest form in this form, free of the prefixes, etc. that distinguish the other forms. The term was adopted to contrast with the terms "heavy" or "כְּבָדִים," which the old Jewish grammarians used to describe the derived forms.

We may quickly determine the general meaning of words by comparing them using a standard, or common measure. Thus, we can be certain that פָּעַל is the form of the third person masculine of all active transitive verbs, פּוֹעֵל of the active participle, we may be certain that שָׁבַר, לָמַד, פָּקַד of the same form, are also of the third person singular masculine; and that שׁוֹבֵר, לוֹמֵד, פּוֹקֵד are participles active; and שָׁבוּר, לָמוּד, פָּקוּד participles passive. Furthermore, we deduce that יָבֵשׁ, זָקֵן are intransitives right away as we know that the form פָּעֵל generally pertains to intransitive verbs; the same goes for every other form of the verb.

Noun forms can also be determined in this way: by comparing them with a similar form that is derived from פָּעַל or any other word in its most basic form that can be used as a standard measure. It will be immediately apparent that, for example, פָּקַד may represent any word whose vowels are Kamets and Pattah. Therefore, any additions or changes to its vowels, consonants, or both will result in the emergence of additional forms that may severally represent words from other classes, each with distinct meanings or shades of meaning. Similar to the formula in Algebra, these terms are used in this sense to identify entire classes of objects that have the same form. As a result, any nouns with three radicals and Kamets under the first and second, such as חָכָם, דָבָר, זָהָב, and so on, are considered to be of the form פָּקָד. Nouns with Kamets for the first radical and Tseri for the second one, such as זָקֵן, חָצֵר belong to the following form פָּקֵד. Thus, מִשְׁפָּט is of the form מִפְקָד, and מַמְלָכָה of the form מַפְקָרָה, etc.

Unusual Conjugations

Apart from the previously listed conjugations, which are the most common, we occasionally encounter other kinds that are distinguished by a characteristic of meaning, which is appropriate to note here; the paradigm has a comprehensive exhibition of these forms. The main ones among these are as follows:

1. פּוֹעֵל – Poel as סוֹבֵב
2. פּוֹעַל – Poal as סוֹבַב
3. פִּלְפֵּל – Pilpel as סִבְסֵב
4. פֻּלְפַּל – Pulpal as סֻבְסַב
5. הִתְפַּלֵּל – Hitpallel as הִתְסַבֵּב
6. הִתְפּוֹלֵל – Hitpilel as הִתְסוֹבֵב

Thus, no one verb is discovered, and most likely never was, showing all the different phases relevant to the conjugations stated above; however, this is an insignificant occurrence because our goal is just to demonstrate the analogical forms of verbs. We won't think twice about providing samples of forms for which there are no real-world examples.

Forms and Meanings of the Usual Conjugations

1. KAL:

קָטַל is the usual form of Kal, where Kamets is under the first radical and Pattah is beneath the second. Generally, the roots of this form are active and transitive, such as שָׁמַר to keep, קָבַר to bury, שָׁפַט to judge; but occasionally they can be intransitive, such in the cases עָמַד to stand, גָּדַל to be great, חָזַק to be strong.

The other forms of roots in Kal are with final Tseri and Cholem, as זָקֵן to be old, יָגֹר to fear; these are almost always intransitive, expressing either quality as נָעֵם which means "to be pleasant or agreeable", טָהֵר to be pure, שָׁפֵל to be humble, יָכֹל to be able; or an affection of mind, as חָפֵץ to be delighted, שָׂנֵא to hate, יָרֵא to fear; or a state of being which excludes the idea of action, as חָסֵר to be in want, רָעֵב to hunger, צָמֵא to thirst, שָׁכֹל to be bereaved.

It should be noted that often the transitive and intransitive, or more accurately the passive, meanings are combined under one form. For example, נָפֵץ means to scutter and to be scattered, שָׁכֵן means to inhabit, and to be inhabited, and אוּץ means to press and to be pressed. This however is rare.

2. NIPHAL:

The appropriate form of Niphal is נִקְטַל. It is created by prefixing Nun with short Chireq (Chireq Qatan) to the ground-form of Kal and dropping the first vowel of the same. Sheva would be the proper pointing of the prefix Nun נְ. However, as this is not allowed, short Chireq is used in its place or by an equivalent vowel in cases where the initial radical is a guttural.

The majority of the time, Niphal's meaning is passive of Kal; for example: שָׁבַר to break, נִשְׁבַּר to be broken, פָּקַד to visit, נִפְקַד to be visited, and sometimes also of Piel and Hiphil. It is frequently just reflexive; fpr example: as נִשְׁמַר to take heed to one's self, נִשְׁאַל to ask for one's self, נִסְתַּר to hide one's self.

Even though neuter verbs aren't strictly speaking capable of being in the passive, there are still a few examples of verbs that fit this description that occur in the passive form. These verbs, however, usually indicate a transition from one state to another, for example: from הָיָה he was, נִהְיָה he became, or was made to be; from חָלָה to be sick, נֶחֱלָה to be made to be sick; and from הָלַךְ to go, to נֶהְלַךְ to go.

A few words in Niphal seem to have an active meaning; for example, נִשְׁבַּע he swore, נִלְחַם he fought, and נֶאֱנַח he sighed. However, even in these instances, the passive import can be discerned, as one who swears (judicially) is at the same time sworn; and one who fights is also fought against; and נֶאֱנַח literally means to become eased, the physical result of sighing.

With the help of our English auxiliaries, Niphal is often translated as can, may, must, ought, could, would, should, etc. Examples of this include יֵאָכֵל that can be eaten, לֹא יִסָּפֵר that cannot be numbered, and לֹא יֵעָשׂוּ that ought not to be done.

3. PIEL:

Piel's characteristic form is קִטֵּל, where Dagesh Forte doubles the second letter and short Chireq and Tseri are assumed in place of Kamets and Pattah. The doubling of the second radical, which often conveys the concept of strengthening, indicates that Piel is typically intensive of Kal in meaning. Thus, Kal שָׁבַר to break, Piel שִׁבֵּר to shatter, or break violently in pieces; שָׁאַל to ask, שִׁאֵל to beg earnestly; נָגַע to touch, נִגַּע to smite.

Thus, in its overall meaning, it means carrying out Kal's instructions with unusual fervour, vigour, energy, and frequency; רָדַף to follow, רִדֵּף to pursue as a persecutor; שָׁלַח to send, שִׁלֵּח to dismiss; צָחַק to laugh, צִחֵק to mock; כָּתַב to write, כִּתֵּב to make a living off of writing.

Piel has a causative, permissive, or declarative, sense in many cases; for example, לָמַד to learn, לִמֵּד to cause that another learns, to instruct; יָלַד to beget, יִלֵּד to aid; חָיָה to live, חִיָּה to permit to live; צָדַק to be just, צִדֵּק to make just, that is, to declare just, to justify; טָמֵא to be impure, טִמֵּא to pronounce unclean. This is consistent with Hiphil's primary significance. Furthermore, Piel frequently turns verbs that are intransitive in Kal into transitive ones, such as אָבַד to perish, אִבֵּד to destroy; חָכַם to be wise, חִכֵּם to make wise; קָדַשׁ to be holy, קִדֵּשׁ to consecrate. In a few instances, it has a privative or opposite meaning in respect to Kal; for example, סָקַל to stone, סִקֵּל to remove stones; נָכַר to know, נִכֵּר to misapprehend; חָטָא to sin, חִטֵּא to expiate sin; הִשְׁרִישׁ (Hiphil) to take root, שֵׁרֵשׁ to eradicate.

4. PUAL:

Pual's characteristic form is קֻטַּל, where Dagesh is similar to Piel but Paul has Kibbuts and Pattah for its initial and terminal vowels. Sometimes Kamets Hateph appears as the first vowel instead of Kibbuts.

Pual is usually often only Piel's passive in meaning, meaning that שֻׁבַּר to be violently broken. In a very few instances it is used as the passive of Kal, for example: לֻקַּח to be taken, of which the Piel form לִקַּח is never used.

5. HIPHIL:

The form הִקְטִיל is the typical form of Hiphil, which has the preformative ה with short Chireq, and inserts Yod with long Chireq between the two final radicals.

Hiphil's primary meaning is causative of Kal; for example, צָרַק to be just, הִצְדִיק to make just or to justify; קָצַף to be enraged, הִקְצִיף to agitate or infuriate; קָדַשׁ to be holy, הִקְדִישׁ to sanctify. This form is so similar to Piel that the same verb appears in both forms very infrequently, and when it does, it's with some slight variation of meaning; for example, כָּבַר to be heavy, כִּבֵּד to honour, הִכְבִּיד to make or pronounce honourable; עָבַר to pass over (as a river), עִבֵּר to transgress a rule, and הֶעֱבִיר to cause to pass over. It can be intransitive at times and sometimes coincides with Kal; for example: עָשַׁר and הֶעֱשִׁיר to berich; שִׁחֵת and הִשְׁחִית to corrupt; לָבֵן and הִלְבִין to be white.

6. HOPHAL:

The typical form of Hophal is הָקְטַל and occasionally, though rarely, הֻקְטַל, with the prefix ה having Kamets Hateph or Kibbuts underneath it.

Hophal is typically employed in the passive form of Hiphil; for example, הִשְׁכִּיב to cause to lay down, הָשְׁכַּב to be caused to lie down; הִמְלִיךְ to make a king, הָמְלַךְ to be made a king. However, the Hophal of יָכֹל, which means to be able, is not unlike from Kal in any way.

7. HITHPAEL:

This conjugation has the form הִתְקַטֵּל. It's compounded of the prefix הִתְ and the inf. construct of Piel קַטֵּל. Regarding signification, most of the time, Hithpael is reflective, especially of Piel; for example: קִדֵּשׁ to sanctify, הִתְקַדֵּשׁ to sanctify one's self, חָזַק to strengthen, הִתְחַזֵּק to strengthen one's self; כִּפֵּר to cover or atone for sin, הִתְכַּפֵּר to make atonement for one's self. It also refers to the act of assuming, demonstrating, or seeming to be or do what the verb's ground-form denotes; as חָלָה to be ill, הִתְחַלָּה to feign one's self sick; עָשַׁר to be wealthy, הִתְעַשֵּׁר to act wealthy, to appear to be wealthy; גָּדַל to be great, ה הִתְגַּדֵּל to carry one's self haughtily.

Exercise 10:

1. What is the correct conjugation for the Hebrew verb כ.ת.ב in the Kal form?

   a) כּוֹתֵב (kotev)
   b) כָּתוּב (katuv)
   c) כָּתַב (katav)
   d) כָּתְבָה (katvah)

2. Which option correctly conjugates the Hebrew verb ד.ב.ר in the Piel form?

   a) דּוֹבֵר (dover)
   b) מְדַבֵּר (medaber)
   c) דִּבֵּר (diber)
   d) דֹּבֵר (dover)

3. What is the correct conjugation for the Hebrew verb ק.ר.א in the Kal form?

   a) קוֹרֵא (kore)
   b) נִקְרָא (nikra)
   c) קָרָא (kara)
   d) נִקְרָא (nikra)

4. Which option correctly conjugates the Hebrew verb ר.פ.א in the Pual form?

   a) נִרְפָּה (nirpa)
   b) רֻפָּה (rupa)
   c) נִרְפָּה (nirpa)
   d) רָפָה (rapha)

5. What is the correct conjugation for the Hebrew verb ק.נ.ה in the Kal form?

   a) הָקְנָה (hokna)
   b) קָנָה (kana)
   c) נִקְנָה (nikna)
   d) קִנֶּה (kineh)

6. Complete the sentence: The Hebrew verb כ.ת.ב in the Kal form is "..............".

7. Fill in the blank: The Piel form of the Hebrew verb ד.ב.ר is "..............".

8. Complete the sentence: In the Hithpael form, the Hebrew verb פ.ל.ל is "..............".

9. Fill in the blank: The Kal form of the Hebrew verb ש.ת.ה is "..............".

10. Complete the sentence: The Hebrew verb ק.ר.א in the Kal form is "..............".

11. Fill in the blank: In the Piel form, the Hebrew verb ב.ד.ק is "..............".

12. Fill in the blank: The Kal form of the Hebrew verb א.כ.ל is "..............".

13. Fill in the blank: The Piel form of the Hebrew verb ר.ק.ד is "..............".

Unusual Conjugations

1. POEL, POAL, and HITHPOEL:

Most of these bear a clear resemblance to Piel in terms of both form and meaning. They have a common inflectional pattern and in several of the irregular verbs occupy the same place. Many of them also have a reflexive form, which is distinguished by the performative הִתְ, much as Piel gives rise to its reflexive Hithpael. Poel, Poal, and Hithpoel are the most common. In meaning, they are frequently, like Piel, causative of Kal, and occasionally they are only tantamount to it; for example: חָקַק and חוֹקֵק, both mean "to give laws". When Piel is used, they might have the same meaning, for example: רִצֵּץ and רוֹצֵץ, both mean "to opress". Frequently, nevertheless, there are noticeable variations between them; for example, סִבֵּב means to turn one's self, סוֹבֵב to go round, to encompass; חִנֵּן to make gracious, חוֹנֵן to compassionate, and שֵׁרֵשׁ to eradicate, שׁוֹרֵשׁ to take root.

2. PILEL, PULAL, and HITHPALEL:

These conjugations are characterized by the doubling of the final radical, with an intervening Tseri or Pattah, based on the analogy of Piel or Pual; such as: קְטָלֵל, קֻטְלַל, הִתְקַטְלֵל. Examples of regular verbs of such conjugations are: שַׁאֲנַן to be quiet, רַעֲנַן to be green, and אֻמְלַל to be withered (passive), none of which have the original roots used שָׁאַן, רָעַן, אָמַל. These conjugations are most commonly used to the verbs Ayin Vav instead of Piel and Hithpael.

3. PILPEL, POLPAL, PEALAL, PEOLEL, and TIPHEL:

It will hardly be sufficient to show the forms of these extremely rare conjugations, of which the general import is intensive and which are, in reality, merely substitutes for the Dageshed conjugations; for example: בִסְבֵס, לִכַלְכָּ or (לִכַלְכֵּ), לְטַלְטֵק, לְטוֹטֵק, לִטְקְתִּ. In flexion, they conform to general analogy.

Modes and Tenses

1. Modes:

Compared to most other languages, Hebrew has a less defined Mode system. Typically, though, three are considered: the indicative, infinitive, and imperative. The indicative is effectively the same as the past or preterite tense, from which it has no distinguishing form, but the two latter are indicated by appropriate forms.

There are two versions of this mode: the construct, a) the absolute, with Kamets and Holem, such as: קָטוֹל, and b) the construct, with Sheva and Holem, such as: קְטֹל. For the specific uses of these two forms, as well as and the reasons of their distinctive appellations, please see the following:

The Infinitive:

a) **Infinitive Absolute:** Typically, this is used with a finite tense of the same verb for the purpose of expressing intensity, assurance, certainty, habitual behaviour, etc. Examples of such cases include: מוֹת תָּמוּת dying you shall die; טָרֹף טֹרַף he is certainly ripped in pieces; הֲמָלֹךְ תִּמְלֹךְ Will you surely reign?; וַיְבָרֶךְ בָּרוֹךְ אֶתְכֶם he kept blessing you; וַיֵּצֵא יָצוֹא וָשׁוֹב and it kept going and coming back.

For any mood, tense, or person, the infinitive absolute can occasionally be employed in place of a finite verb; for example, 'The living creatures רָצוֹא וָשׁוֹב ran and returned, זָכוֹר אֶת־ יוֹם הַשַּׁבָּת remember the Sabbath day, מָרַדְנוּ וְסוֹר we have rebelled and apostatized. וְאֶתְכֶם הוֹצִיא מִתּוֹכָהּ and I will bring you out of the midst of her, Fields shall they buy, וְכָתוֹב and they shall write bills of sale, וְחָתוֹם and they shall seal them, וְהָעֵר and take witnesses.

In some cases, the infinitive absolute might have an adverbial sense or a sense similar to the Latin gerund. For example, הָחֵל וְכַלֵּה which means "utterly"; the verse reads: אָלֹה וְכַחֵשׁ וְרָצֹחַ וְגָנֹב וְנָאֹף פָּרָצוּ by cursing, and dissembling, and murdering, and stealing, and committing adultery they break out.

In some few instances, the Infinitive form is used absolutely in the strictest sense of the term, meaning that it does not rely on any other word; an example of this would be, "The Lord made a covenant with Abraham, לֵאמֹר saying, etc."

b) **Infinitive Construct:** The Infinitive Construct possesses all the essential characteristics of a noun, and it is employed as such in construction, position, government, and form; for example: הֱיוֹת הָאָדָם "the being of the man" alone is not good; עֲשׂת צְדָקָה "the doing of righteousness" is more acceptable; וְהָיוּ לַעֲמֹד And let them be for serving; תִּהְיֶה לְהִבָּקֵעַ it shall be for being pierced through; אַתָּה יָדַעְתָּ שִׁבְתִּי וְקוּמִי you know my down-sitting and my up-rising, בְּבֹא רָשָׁע in the coming of the wicked; I will guard my way מֵחֲטוֹא from sinning; And they returned מִתּוּר הָאָרֶץ from searching of the land.

The Infinitive Constuct in Kal has, like the Preterite, three forms; קְטֹל, שְׁכַב, נְתֵן. For the feminine form of the Infinitive קִטְלָה, קָטְלָה, קְטֹלָה, etc.

Peculiar use of the Infinitive construct with לְ:

The easiest way to explain this is with examples, such as: וַיְהִי הַשֶּׁמֶשׁ לָבוֹא the sun was about to set; "He that is wise טוֹב לִמְצֹא (is) for finding prosperity"; יְהוָה לְהוֹדִיעָם Jehovah will be for the teaching of them; יְהוָה לְהוֹשִׁיעֵנִי Jehovah will be for the delivering of me; "And it came to pass וְהַשַּׁעַר לִסְגּוֹר at the shutting of the gate, i.e. when the gate was to be shut; מֶה לַעֲשׂוֹת what (is) to be done for you?; הֲלָרָשָׁע לַעְזֹר should one help the wicked?; לֹא לְהוֹרִישׁ he could not dispossess them.

Both the Accusative of the object and the Genitive of the subject are found to be in relation to the Infinitive construct; for example, בְּיוֹם עֲשׂוֹת יְהוָה אֶרֶץ וְשָׁמַיִם in the day of Jehovah's creation of the earth and the heavens; יוֹם עַנּוֹת אָדָם נַפְשׁוֹ a the day of a man's afflicting his soul; בִּשְׁמֹעַ הַמֶּלֶךְ אֶת־דְּבַר־אִישׁ to speak in the king's hearing of the man's word; בְּפָתְחִי אֶת־קִבְרוֹתֵיכֶם in my opening of your graves.

The Imperative:

The form of the imperative usually corresponds to the infinitive construct of the same conjugation; for example, קְטֹל to kill, קְטֹל kill you.

The imperative is only used in positive precepts, prayers, and exhortations. The future is always used in negative precepts, prohibitions, exhortations, and deprecations. For example, the phrase לֹא תִּרְצָח you shall not kill, instead of לֹא רְצַח kill you not.

The future, occasionally in a somewhat modified form, is used to indicate the subjunctive and optative modes.

2. Tenses:

The Preterite and the Future are the only two tenses. In order to indicate person and gender, the Preterite is denoted by appending pronoun fragments to the root (the third person singular masculine. For example:

	Singular		
Masculine		קָטַל	Ground-form
Feminine	ה.....	קָטְלָ-ה	Fragment of הִיא
Masculine	תָּ.....	קָטַלְ-תָּ	Fragment of אַתָּה
Feminine	תְּ.....	קָטַלְ־תְּ	Fragment of אַתְּ
Masculine & Feminine	תִּי.....	קָטַלְ-תִּי	Derivation unknown
	Plural		
Masculine & Feminine	וּ.....	קָטְלְ-וּ	Derivation unknown
Masculine	תֶּם.....	קְטַלְ־תֶּם	Fragment of אַתֶּם
Feminine	תֶּן.....	קְטַלְ־תֶּן	Fragment of אַתֶּן
Masculine & Feminine	נוּ	קָטַלְנוּ	Fragment of אֲנוּ

Prefixes and suffixes appended to its ground-form, commonly regarded as the Infinitive construct, are used to denote the Future. For example:

	Singular		
Masculine	יִ-קְטֹל	Without disjunction	יִקְטֹל
Feminine	תִּ-קְטֹל	Without disjunction	תִּקְטֹל
Masculine	תִּ-קְטֹל	Without disjunction	תִּקְטֹל
Feminine	תִּ-קְטְלִ-י	Without disjunction	תִּקְטְלִי
Masculine & Feminine	אֶ-קְטֹל	Without disjunction	אֶקְטֹל

Plural			
Masculine	יִ-קְטְל-וּ	Without disjunction	יִקְטְלוּ
Feminine	תִּ-קְטוּלְ-נָה	Without disjunction	תִּקְטוּלְנָה
Masculine	תִּ-קְטְל-וּ	Without disjunction	תִּקְטְלוּ
Feminine	תִּ-קְטֹלְ-נָה	Without disjunction	תִּקְטֹלְנָה
Masculine & Feminine	נִ-קְטֹל	Without disjunction	נִקְטֹל

Either Holem, Pattah, or Tseri is the last vowel in the Future; for example: יִקְטֹל, יִכְבַּד, יֵשֵׁב. These are technically termed Future O, A, and E. The first, or Holem, is the most common of them in regular verbs.

Exercises Answer Key

Exercise 1:

1. a
2. a
3. c
4. a
5. c
6. d
7. Z
8. Pey
9. T
10. M
11. ן
12. R
13. S
14. ך
15. L

Exercise 2:

1. a
2. c
3. d
4. b
5. Kametz
6. Chireq
7. Tseri
8. Segol
9. Shureq
10. Patach

Exercise 3:

1. d
2. b
3. d
4. doubling

Exercise 4:

1. a
2. a
3. c
4. c

Exercise 5:

1. c
2. b
3. c
4. c
5. גְּדוֹלָה
6. סְפָרִים
7. אִישִׁים
8. עֵרִים
9. בָּתִּים

Exercise 6:

1. a
2. d
3. c
4. a
5. a
6. חֲמִישִׁי – חֲמִישִׁית
7. שִׁבְעָה – שֶׁבַע
8. עֶשֶׂר – עֶשְׂרֵה
9. אַחַד עָשָׂר - אַחַת עֶשְׂרֵה
10. חֲמִשִּׁים
11. תְּשִׁיעִי – תְּשִׁיעִית
12. שָׁלוֹשׁ – שְׁלוֹשָׁה
13. שִׁשִּׁים וְאַרְבָּעָה
14. מֵאָה
15. טוֹב יוֹתֵר
16. יָפֶה בְּיוֹתֵר
17. שְׂמַח יוֹתֵר

Exercise 7:

1. b
2. d
3. a
4. b
5. c
6. c
7. אַתֶּם
8. אֲנִי
9. הֵן
10. אֲנַחְנוּ

11. הֵם
12. אַתְּ

Exercise 8:

1. a
2. b
3. a
4. b
5. d
6. a
7. b
8. b
9. לְ
10. from
11. on
12. עִם
13. with

Exercise 9:

1. a
2. b
3. c
4. d
5. d
6. c
7. c
8. וְ
9. or
10. explanation - reason
11. כִּי
12. if
13. also
14. contrast - contradiction
15. but
16. concessive clauses

Exercise 10:

1. c
2. c
3. c
4. b
5. b
6. כָּתַב
7. דִּבֵּר
8. הִתְפַּלֵּל
9. שָׁתָה
10. קָרָא
11. בִּדֵּק
12. אָכַל
13. רִקֵּד

Hebrew Phrasebook For *Beginners*

Learn Common Phrases in Context with Explanations for Everyday Use and Travel

Welcome to your journey of Hebrew basics! We've kept things practical and useful in this phrasebook to help you get started in your first Hebrew talks. Don't bother about extensive vocabulary or intricate grammatical rules; simply focus on the basics.

This phrasebook will cover the fundamentals of travelling, including how to communicate with people in Hebrew, find hotels and dining options, and even what to say in an emergency. Having this phrasebook on hand will be essential to having a worry-free Hebrew holiday and making the most of your interactions with the locals!

Chapter 1
Formality

Hebrew does not differentiate between formal and informal speech. This means that you will address every person you meet with the 2nd person singular. Remember to modify gender according to who you're addressing. You will also modify your address if you're speaking to more than one person.

Useful Vocabulary and Phrases

Here are some useful vocabularies and phrases to use in everyday life below. Enjoy your learning!

Greetings:

Hello! Hi!	Shalom	שלום
Goodbye!	Shalom, lehitraot	שלום, להתראות
Good morning	Boker tov	בוקר טוב
Good afternoon	Tsohoraim tovim	צהריים טובים
Good evening	Erev tov	ערב טוב
Good night!	Laila tov	לילה טוב!
See you later!	Lehitraot	להתראות!
Yes	Ken	כן
No	Lo	לא
Thank you!	Toda	תודה
Thank you very much!	Toda raba	תודה רבה!
You're welcome!	Al lo davar	על לא דבר!
Please give me	Bevaksha ten li	בבקשה תן לי ....
The ticket	Et hakartis	את הכרטיס
My passport	Et hadarkon	את הדרכון שלי
Sorry	slicha	סליחה!
Excuse me, please!	Slach li bevakasha	סלח לי בבקשה
How are you?	Eych ata margish	איך אתה מרגיש?
Ok	Beseder	בסדר
Sit down!	Shev	שב!
I don't know	Ani lo yodea	אני לא יודע
I don't speak English	Ani lo medaber(et) anglit	אני לא מדבר(ת) אנגלית
Do you speak Hebrew?	Ata medaber ivrit?	אתה מדבר עברית?
My name is	Shmi	שמי ....
What's your name?	Ma shimcha (shmech)?	מה שמך?
I'd like to introduce you to	Takir (takiri) bevakasha et	תכיר(י) בבקשה את ....

I'm pleased to meet you	Na'im me'od	נעים מאוד
Do you live here?	Ata (at) gar (gara) kan?	אתה/את גר/גרה כאן?
Are you here on holiday?	Ata (at) kan bechufsha?	אתה (את) כאן בחופשה?
How long are you here for?	Lekama zman bata (bat)	לכמה זמן באת?
I'm/We're here for .... weeks/days.	I'm/We're here for .... weeks/days	אני/אנחנו פה .... שבועות/ ימים.
I'm here on/to	Ani kan le	אני כאן ל ....

Chapter 2
Getting around

How do we get to ....?	Eich mag'im le ....?	איך מגיעים ל ....?
Is it far from/near here?	Ha'im ze rachok mikan/karov lekan?	האם זה רחוק מכאן/קרוב לכאן?
Can we walk there?	Efshar lalechet lesham baregel?	אפשר ללכת לשם ברגל?
Can you show me on the map?	Ata yachol (at yechola) lehar'ot li al hamapa?	אתה יכול (את יכולה) להראות לי על המפה?
Are there other means of getting to ....?	Efshar lehagi'a le .... badrachim acherot?	אפשר להגיע ל .... בדרכים אחרות?
Where can I buy a ticket?	Eifo efshar liknot kartisim?	איפה אפשר לקנות כרטיסים?
We want to go to	Anakhno rotsim linso'a le	אנחנו רוצים לנסוע ל ....
Do I need to book?	Tsarich lehazmin makom merosh?	צריך להזמין מקום מראש?
I'd like to book a seat to	Ani rotse lehazmin makom le	אני אוצה להזמין מקום ל ....
Can I get a stand-by ticket?	Efshar liknot kartis stand-by?	אפשר לקנות כרטיס סטנד-ביי?
Is there a flight to ....?	Yesh tisa le ....?	יש טיסה ל ....?
Where is the next flight to ....?	Matay hatisa haba'a le ....?	מתי הטיסה הבאה ל ....?
How long does the flight take?	Ma meshech hatisa?	מה משך הטיסה?
What time do I have to check in at the airport?	Matay alai lavo lisde hate'ufa?	מתי עלי לבוא לשדה התעופה?
What time does the plane leave/arrive?	Matay mamri/nochet ha'aviron?	מתי ממריא/נוחת האווירון?
Where's the baggage claim?	Eifo masof hamizvadot?	איפה מסוף המזוודות?
Where is the bus station?	Eifo hatchana hamerkazit?	איפה התחנה המרכזית?
Which bus goes to ....?	Eize otobus nose'a le ....?	איזה אוטובוס נוסע ל ....?
Does this bus go to ....?	Haotobus haze nose'a le ....?	האוטובוס הזה נוסע ל ....?
What time does the bus leave/arrive?	Matay yotse/magi'a ha'otobus?	מתי יוצא מגיע האוטובוס?
How often do buses come?	Ma tchifut ha'otobus?	מה תכיפות האוטובוס?
Could you let me know when we get to ....?	Ata yachol (at yechola) lomar li keshengi'a le ....?	אתה יכול (את יכולה) לאמר לי כשנגיע ל ....?
Where do I get the bus for ....?	Eifo ha'otobus le ....?	איפה האוטובוס ל ....?
Where's the train station?	Eifo takhanat ha'rakevet?	איפה תחנת הרכבת?

Does this train stop at . . . .?	Harakevet otseret be . . . .?	הרכבת עוצרת ב . . . .?
What time does the train leave/arrive?	Matay yotset/magi'a harakevet?	מתי יוצאת/מגיעה הרכבת?
I want to get off at	Ani rotse (rotsa) laredet be	אני רוצה לרדת ב . . . .
How much does it cost to go to . . . .?	Kama ola hanesi'a le . . . .?	כמה עולה הנסיעה ל . . . .?
How much is the fare?	Ma hamechir?	מה המחיר?
Please take me to	Bevakasha sa le	בבקשה סע ל . . . .

Chapter 3
Hotels and Accommodations

I'm looking for a	Ani mechabes(et)	אני מחפש(ת) ....
Where can I find a .... hotel?	Eifo yesh malon ....?	איפה יש מלון ....?
Where's the .... hotel?	Eifo hamalon .... beyoter?	איפה המלון .... ביותר?
What's the address?	Ma haktovet?	מה הכתובת?
Could you write me down the address, please?	Ata yachol (at yechola) lirshom li et haktovet bevakasha?	אתה יכול (את יכולה) לרשום לי את הכתובת בבקשה?
I'd like to book a room please	Ani rotse (rotsa) lehazmin cheder bevakasha	אני רוצה להזמין חדר בבקשה
Do you have any rooms available?	Yesh chadarim pnuyim?	יש חדרים פנויים?
We'll be arriving at	Nagi'a be	נגיע ב ....
Do you have a room with two beds?	Yesh cheder im shtei mitot?	יש חדר עם שתי מיטות?
Do you have a room with a double bed?	Yesh cheder im mita kfula?	יש חדר עם מיטה כפולה?
We want a room with a	Anachnu rotsim cheder im	אנחנו רוצים חדר עם ....
I need a	Anu tsarich (tsricha)	אני צריך (צריכה) ....

Chapter 4
Health

I need a/an	Ani tsarikh	אני צריך ....
Doctor	Rofe	רופא
Hospital	Beit Cholim	בית חולים
Emergency room	Chadar miyun	חדר מיון
Ambulance	Magen David adom	מגן דוד אדום
Nurse	Achot	אחות
Medicine	Trufa	תרופה
I feel a	Ngani margish .... keev	אני מרגיש כאב ....
I have a/an	Yesh li	יש לי ....
Ear, ears	Ozen, oznaim	אוזן, אוזנים
Eye, eyes	Ain, eynaim	עין, עיניים
Hand, hand	Yad, yadaim	יד, ידים
Head	Rosh	ראש
Heart	Lev	כן
Leg, legs	regel, regalaim	רגל, רגלים
Problem with	Baaya im	בעיה עם ....
Stomach	Beten	בטן
(High) temperature	Chom	חום
Wound	Petsa	פצע
I have	Yesh li	יש לי ....
Skin	Or	עור
Hair	Saarot	שערות
Nails	Tsipornaim	ציפורניים
He, she was	Hi haya, hi hayta	הוא היה, היא היתה ....
Unconscious	Lelo hakara	ללא הכרה
Wounded	Patsua, ptsua	פצוע, פצועה
In a road accident	Beteunat drachim	בתאונת דרכים
I have to	Ani hayav	אני חייב ....
Contact	lehitkasher	להתקשר
Call	Likro le	לקרוא ל ....
Phone	Letsaltsel	לצלצל
Enter	Lehikanes	להיכנס
Come	Lavo	לבוא
This must	Ze tsarich	זה צריך ....
Be right	Lihyot nachon	להיות נכון
I'm sick	Any chole (chola)	אני חולה
My .... hurts	Ko'ev li	כואב לי ....

I feel better/worse	Ani margish(a) yoter tov/raa	אני מרגיש(ה) יותר טוב/רע
I feel under the weather	Ani margish(a) lo kmo atsmi	אני מרגיש(ה) לא כמו עצמי
I feel nauseous	Yesh li bchila	יש לי בחילה
This is my usual medicine	Zo hatrufa she'ani loke'ach (lokachat)	זו התרופה שאני לוקח (לוקחת)
I'm pregnant	Ani beherayon	אני בהיריון
I have a skin allergy	Yesh li tguva alergit ba'or	יש לי תגובה אלרגית בעור
I'm on medications for	Ani mekabel(let) trufor neged	אני מקבל(ת) תקופות נגד . . . .
I need something for	Ani tsarich (tsaricha) mashehu le	אני צריך (צריכה) משהו ל . . . .
I need a prescription for	Ani tsarich (tsaricha) mirsham bishvil	אני צריך (צריכה) מרשם בשביל . . . .

Chapter 5
Shopping

Rate	Taarif	תעריף
Shop	Chanut	חנות
Sale	Mchira	מכירה
Salesman	Moocher	מוכר
Saleswoman	Mocheret	מוכרת
Price	Mchir	מחיר
Discount	Hanacha	הנחה
Sale	mivtsa	מבצע
Gifts/Presents	Matanot	מתנות
Souvenir store	Chanut mazkerot	חנות מזכרות
Jewelry store	Chanut tachshitim	חנות תכשיטים
Supermarket	Supermarket	סופרמרקט
Supersal (name of supermarket	Supersal	שופרסל
Shekem (name of store)	Shekem	שקם
Book store	Chanut sfarim	חנות ספרים
Book (books)	Sefer (sfarim)	ספר (ספרים)
Newspaper (newspapers)	Iton (itonim)	עיתון (עיתונים)
market	Shuk	שוק
Where can I but ....?	Eifo efshar liknot ....?	איפה אפשר לקנות ....?
Where's the nearest ....?	Eifo ha .... hakarov (hakrova)?	איפה ה .... הקרוב (הקרובה)?
I'd like to buy	Ani rotse (rotsa) liknot	אני רוצה לקנות ....
Do you have others?	Yesh acherim?	יש אחרים?
I don't like it	Ani lo ohev(et) et ze	אני לא אוהב(ת) את זה
Can I look at ....?	Ani yachol (yechola) lehistakel ba ....?	אני יכול (יכולה) להסתכל ב ....?
I'd like	Ani rotse (rotsa)	אני רוצה ....
Where can I find ....?	Eifo efshar limtso ....?	איפה אפשר למצוא ....?
I'm just looking	Ani rak mistakel(et)	אני רק מסתכל(ת)
How much is this?	Kama ze ale?	כמה זה עולה?
Can you write down the price?	Ata yachol lirshom et hamachir al daf?	אתה יכול לרשום את המחיר על הדף?
Do you accept credit cards?	Efshar leshalem bekartis ashra'i?	אפשר לשלם בכרטיס אשראי?
Please wrap it	Bevakasha la'atof	בבקשה לעטוף

I think it's too expensive	Ani choshev(et) sheze yoter miday yakar	אני חושב(ת) שזה מידי יקר
It's too much for us	Ze yoter miday yakar bishvilenu	זה יותר מידי יקר בישבילנו
Can you lower the price?	Efshar lekabel hanacha?	אפשר לקבל הנחה?

Chapter 6
Restaurants and Eating out

Kosher Food/law is a system of food categorization based on biblical precepts which is called Kashrut, or Kosher law. Land animals with cloven hooves and cud chewing habits fall under the kosher classification. Animals raised according to Kosher standards are killed in a way so that no blood remains in their meat. Seafood that is Kosher has to have fins and scales.

Milk (also known as "Chalav") cannot be consumed with or used to prepare or consume meat (also known as "Baser"). Fish and eggs are examples of "neutral" foods that may be eaten with either milk or meat.

If only Jews are engaged in the manufacturing of the wine, it is considered Kosher. Because Kosher wine is so sacred, it loses its Kosher status if a non-Jew looks-upon an open bottle.

Wine is first boiled in order to make it acceptable for people of other faiths to drink it during religious ceremonies. Despite Israel's reputation as the "land of milk and honey", was not always regarded as Kosher. A lot of biblical historians think that the word "honey" really refers to "date jam", however, the designation of honey as Kosher developed over time.

I'm a vegetarian	Ani tsimchoni(t)	אני צמחוני(ת)
I don't eat	Ani lo ochel(et)	אני לא אוכל ....
Do you have any vegetarian dishes?	Yes lachem ma'achalim tismchoni'im?	יש לכם מאכלים צמחוניים?
Does this dish have ....?	Yesh .... bama'achal haze?	יש .... במאכל הזה?
Can I get this without ....?	Efshar lekabel et hamana hazot bli ....?	אפשר לקבל את המנה הזרת בלי ....?
I'm allergic to	Ani alergi(t) le	אני אלרגי(ת) ל ....
Is there a kosher restaurant here?	Yesh mis'ada kshera bsviva?	יש מסעדה כשרה בסביבה?
Table for ...., please	Shulchan le ...., bevakasha	שולחן ל ....,. בבקשה
May we see the menu?	Efshar lir'ot et hatafrit?	אפשר לראות את התפריט?
Please bring some	Bevakasha tavi kama	בבקשה תביא כמה ....
No ice in my ...., please	Bli kerach ba .... sheli, bevakasha	בלי קרח ב .... שלי, בבקשה

Chapter 7
Sports and Hobbies

What do you do in your spare time?	Ma ata ose bizmancha hapanui?	מה אתה עושה בזמנך הפנוי?
I like to	Ani ohev(et)	אני אוהב(ת) . . . .
Do you like . . . .?	Ata ohev . . . .?	אתה אוהב . . . .?
I like playing sport	Ani ohev(et) la'asot sport	אני אוהב(ת) לעשות ספורט
Do you play . . . .?	Ata mesachek . . . .?	אתה משחק . . . .?
Can we swim here?	Mutar lischot po?	מותר לשחות פה?
We'd like to hire diving equipment	Anachnu rotsim liskor tsiyud tslila	אנחנו רוצים לשכור ציוד צלילה
Art	Omanut	אמנות
Dancing	Rikudim	ריקודים
Cooking	Bishul	בישול
Film	Seret	סרט
Music	Musika	מוסיקה
Going out	Latset levalot	לצאת לבלות
Playing games	Lesachek mischakim	לשחק משחקים
Playing soccer	Lesachek kaduregel	לשחק בכדורגל
Playing sport	La'asot sport	לעשות ספורט
Reading books	Likro sfarim	לקרוא ספרים
Shopping	La'asot shopping	לעשות שופינג
Travelling	Letayel	לטייל
Watching TV	Lir'ot televisia	לראות טלוויזיה
Photography	Tsilum	צילום
The theatre	Tearron	תיאטרון
Writing	Ktiva	כתיבה

Hebrew Short Stories For Language Learners

Learn and Improve Your Hebrew Comprehension Through 20 Short Stories

1. אמונת האיכר: סיפור על השגחה אלוהית

בארץ ישראל הקדומה, בתקופה שבה שלטו מלכים ונביאים דיברו את דבר ה', חי איכר צנוע בשם אלי. אלי עבד את שדות אבותיו הפוריים, עבד את האדמה וזרע זרעים בזהירות, בוטח בהשגחת הקב"ה שיברך את יבוליו.

שנה אחת, בצורת גדולה ירדה על הארץ, והשדות הירוקים של פעם הפכו יבשים ועקרים. אנשי הכפר הפכו נואשים, חנויותיהם הצטמצמו ותקוותיהם נמוגות עם כל יום שעובר. אבל אלי נשאר איתן באמונתו, מאמין שאלוהים יפרנס אותו ואת משפחתו.

כשהימים נמשכו לשבועות והשבועות לחודשים, אלי המשיך לטפל בשדותיו, מתפלל בלהט לגשם שיכבה את האדמה היבשה. למרות הספקנות של שכניו ולחישות הספק שאפפו אותו, אלי נשאר נחוש, בוטח בהבטחת רחמי ה'.

ואז, לילה אחד, כשאלי שכב ישן במעונו הצנוע, ביקר אותו חזון. בחלומו הופיע לפניו מלאך ה', שטוף באור זוהר שהאיר את החושך. המלאך דיבר אל אלי בקול שנראה כמו מהדהד מהשמים עצמם, ואמר: "אל תירא כי שמע ה' את תפילותיך וראה את נאמנותך. צא מחר וזרע שוב את שדותיך כי יבואו הגשמים. ותשוב הארץ".

בלב מלא תקווה והכרת תודה, התעורר אלי מחלומו ויצא לשדותיו כשאור השחר הראשון צובע את השמיים. בכל צעד שעשה, הוא הרגיש תחושת שלווה וביטחון שוטפים אותו, בידיעה שאלוהים איתו ושתפילותיו נשמעו.

כשאלי עיבד את האדמה, ידיו מונחות על ידי אמונה ולבו מורם בתפילה, הוא הרגיש רוח עדינה מתחילה להתסיס, נושאת עימה את ריח הגשם. עננים כהים נאספו באופק, ורעם רעם מרחוק, ובישר את בואו של הגשם המיוחל.

כשדמעות שמחה זולגות על פניו, אלי הרים את מבטו לשמים והודה לאל על חסדו וחסדו. הגשם ירד בזרמים, ספג את האדמה והחזיר חיים לשדות שהיו פעם עקרים. אנשי הכפר שמחו, רוחם התרוממת בעקבות השתלשלות העניינים המופלאה.

מאותו יום ואילך, אמונתו והתמדה של אלי הפכו לאגדות ברחבי הארץ. סיפורו הועבר מדור לדור, עדות לכוחה של התפילה ולאהבת ה' הבלתי פוסקת. ובכל פעם שהתקשו הזמנים, האנשים היו מסתכלים על אלי כדוגמה של איתנות ואמון בשכינה.

וכך, סיפורו של אלי החקלאי נשזר במרקם ההיסטוריה של ישראל, תזכורת לכך שגם בזמנים האפלים ביותר, אמונה יכולה להזיז הרים ועדיין יכולים לקרות ניסים למי שמאמין.

Translation:

The Farmer's Faith: A Story of Divine Providence

In the ancient land of Israel, at a time when kings ruled and prophets spoke the word of God, there lived a humble farmer named Eli. Eli cultivated the fertile fields of his ancestors, tilled the soil and sowed seeds carefully, trusting in the providence of God to bless his crops.

One year, a great drought descended on the land, and the once green fields became dry and barren. The villagers have become desperate, their stores have dwindled and their hopes are fading with each passing day. But Eli remained steadfast in his faith, believing that God would provide for him and his family.

As the days stretched into weeks and the weeks into months, Eli continued tending his fields, fervently praying for rain to quench the dry land. Despite the skepticism of his neighbors and the whispers of doubt that surrounded him, Eli remained determined, trusting in the promise of God's mercy.

Then, one night, as Eli lay asleep in his humble abode, he was visited by a vision. In his dream, an angel of God appeared before him, bathed in a luminous light that illuminated the darkness. The angel spoke to Eli in a voice that seemed to echo from heaven itself, and said: "Do not be afraid because God has heard your prayers and seen your faithfulness. Go out tomorrow and sow your fields again because the rains will come. And the earth will return."

With a heart full of hope and gratitude, Eli woke up from his dream and went out to his fields as the first light of dawn colored the sky. With every step he took, he felt a sense of peace and security wash over him, knowing that God was with him and that his prayers were heard.

As Eli tilled the soil, his hands guided by faith and his heart lifted in prayer, he felt a gentle wind begin to stir, carrying with it the scent of rain. Dark clouds gathered on the horizon, and thunder rumbled in the distance, heralding the coming of the long-awaited rain.

With tears of joy streaming down his face, Eli looked up to heaven and thanked God for his grace and mercy. The rain came down in torrents, soaking the soil and bringing life back to the once barren fields. The people of the village were happy, their spirits were lifted by the wonderful turn of events.

From that day on, Eli's faith and perseverance became legends throughout the country. His story was passed down from generation to generation, a testimony to the power of prayer and God's unceasing love. And whenever times got tough, the people would look to Eli as an example of steadfastness and trust in Shekinah.

And so, the story of Eli the farmer is woven into the fabric of Israel's history, a reminder that even in the darkest times, faith can move mountains and miracles can still happen to those who believe.

2. סיפור על אוצר ואמון

בשוק הומה בירושלים העתיקה, גר סוחר צעיר בשם עזרא. עזרא היה ידוע ברחבי העיר בחוש העסקי הממולח שלו ובכישרונו לבצע עסקאות משתלמות. הוא נסע למרחקים, סחר בסחורות מארצות רחוקות וצבר עושר מעבר לחלומותיו הפרועים ביותר.

למרות הצלחתו, עזרא לא הסתפק. עמוק בתוך לבו, הוא טמן כמיהה להרפתקה ולהתרגשות, רצון להשתחרר מגבולות חייו הנוחים ולחפש אתגרים חדשים.

יום אחד, כשעזרא התכונן לצאת למסע מסחר נוסף, הוא שמע לחישות של חפץ מסתורי שלפי השמועות חבוי עמוק בתוך חולות המדבר. אמרו שהוא בעל כוח ועושר בלתי נספרים, מספיק כדי להגשים אפילו את חלומותיו של הסוחר העשיר ביותר.

מסוקרן מהאפשרות של תגלית כזו, עזרא החליט לצאת למסע חיפוש אחר החפץ האגדי. הוא אסף אספקה, שכר להקה קטנה של מטיילים מנוסים ויצא לדרך אל המדבר העצום, מונחה רק על ידי השמועות הקלושות וההבטחה להרפתקה.

ימים הפכו לשבועות כאשר עזרא וחבריו נסעו עמוק יותר לתוך המדבר, מול פני שטח בוגדניים וחום סוחף. בדיוק כשהחלו לאבד תקווה, הם נתקלו במקדש עתיק שהוסתר בין הדיונות.

בהתרגשות הם נכנסו למקדש, ליבם פועם בציפייה. כאשר חקרו את האולמות העתיקים שלה, הם גילו גילופים המתארים את החפץ שהם חיפשו, ואישרו שהם בדרך הנכונה.

אבל בדיוק כשהם עמדו להגיע אל הקודש הפנימי שבו נאמר שהחפץ מוסתר, הם התעמתו עם להקת שודדים חסרי רחמים שעקבה אחר כל צעד שלהם. התפתח קרב עז, כאשר עזרא וחבריו נלחמו בגבורה כדי להגן על עצמם.

בעיצומו של הכאוס, בן לוויתו המהימן ביותר של עזרא, סייף מיומן בשם יוסף, התגלה כבוגד, לאחר שעבד בסתר עם השודדים כל הזמן. מזועזע ונבגד, עזרא בקושי האמין למראה עיניו כשראה את יוסף פונה נגדם, חברו הנאמן שהיה פעם נלחם כעת לצד אויביהם.

למרות הסיכויים שנערמו נגדם, הצליחו עזרא ושאר חברי מפלגתו לגבור על השודדים ולצאת מנצחים. אבל הבגידה הותירה את חותמה, והטילה צל של ספק וחוסר אמון על הקשר שהיה פעם בלתי שביר ביניהם.

בלב כבד המשיכו עזרא וחבריו במסעם, ובסופו של דבר הגיעו לקודש הקודש הפנימי של המקדש בו חיכה להם החפץ. אבל כשהם הביטו על פני השטח הנוצצים שלו, הבין עזרא שהאוצר האמיתי שחיפש כל הזמן הוא לא עושר או כוח, אלא ידידות ונאמנות.

וכך, עם תחושה חדשה של בהירות ותכלית, קיבל עזרא את ההחלטה לחזור הביתה, והשאיר מאחוריו את הפיתוי של עושר והרפתקאות לטובת הדברים החשובים באמת. כשחזר לירושלים, הוא ידע ששום אוצר לא יוכל להשתוות לערך האג"ח שחלק עם אלה שהוא אוהב.

Translation:

A Story about Treasure and Trust

In a busy market in Old Jerusalem, lived a young merchant named Ezra. Ezra was known throughout the city for his shrewd business acumen and his talent for making lucrative deals. He traveled far and wide, traded goods from distant lands and amassed wealth beyond his wildest dreams.

Despite his success, Ezra was not satisfied. Deep in his heart, he hid a longing for adventure and excitement, a desire to break free from the confines of his comfortable life and seek new challenges.

One day, as Ezra prepared to go on another trading trip, he heard whispers of a mysterious object rumored to be hidden deep within the desert sands. He was said to possess untold power and wealth, enough to make even the richest merchant's dreams come true.

Intrigued by the possibility of such a discovery, Ezra decided to go on a search for the legendary object. He gathered supplies, hired a small band of experienced travelers and set out into the vast desert, guided only by the faintest rumors and the promise of adventure.

Days turned into weeks as Ezra and his friends drove deeper into the desert, facing treacherous terrain and overwhelming heat. Just when they started to lose hope, they came across an ancient temple hidden among the dunes.

Excitedly they entered the temple, their hearts beating in anticipation. When they explored its ancient halls, they discovered carvings depicting the object they were looking for, confirming that they were on the right track.

But just as they were about to reach the inner sanctum where the artifact was said to be hidden, they were confronted by a merciless band of bandits following their every move. A fierce battle ensued, with Ezra and his friends fighting valiantly to defend themselves.

In the midst of the chaos, Ezra's most trusted companion, a skilled swordsman named Yosef, was revealed to be a traitor, having secretly worked with the bandits all along. Shocked and betrayed, Ezra could hardly believe his eyes as he saw Joseph turn against them, his once loyal friend now fighting alongside their enemies.

Despite the odds stacked against them, Ezra and the other members of his party managed to overcome the bandits and emerge victorious. But the betrayal left its mark, casting a shadow of doubt and mistrust over the bond that was once unbreakable between them.

With a heavy heart, Ezra and his friends continued their journey, eventually reaching the inner sanctum sanctorum of the temple where the object awaited them. But as they gazed upon its glittering surface, Ezra realized that the true treasure he had been seeking all along was not wealth or power, but friendship and loyalty.

And so, with a new sense of clarity and purpose, Ezra made the decision to return home, leaving behind the lure of wealth and adventure in favor of the truly important things. When he returned to Jerusalem, he knew that no treasure could match the value of the bond he shared with those he loved.

3. נס בבית אל

פעם, בארץ ישראל העתיקה, היה כפר השוכן בין גבעות מתגלגלות ועמקים עבותים. כפר זה נודע בשם בית אל, ותושביו חיו חיים פשוטים אך מספקים, המודרכים על ידי מסורות שעברו לאורך הדורות.

בבית אל גר זקן חכם בשם רבי אברהם. הוא היה נערץ על ידי כל בכפר על ידיעתו בתורה ואמונתו הבלתי מעורערת באלוהים. רבי אברהם העביר את ימיו ללמד את הצעירים, לייעץ לנפגעים ולהדריך לנזקקים.

ערב אחד, כשרבי אברהם ישב מחוץ למשכנו הצנוע, והביט בכוכבים הנוצצים מלמעלה, ניגש אליו נוסע עייף. שמו של המטייל היה יוסף, והוא נסע מארץ רחוקה בחיפוש אחר תשובות לשאלות העמוקות של החיים.

יוסף הסביר לרבי אברהם ששמע על הכפר בית אל ועל החכם הנודע שלו, והוא מקווה שהרב יוכל להציע לו את החכמה שביקש. רבי אברהם קיבל את יוסף לביתו והאזין בקשב רב כשהנוסע שפך את ליבו.

יוסף דיבר על התמודדויותיו וספקותיו, על הניסיונות שעמד בפניהם במסעו ועל הריקנות שחש בפנים. הוא השתוקק למצוא משמעות ותכלית בחייו, להבין את מקומו בעולם ואת יחסיו עם האלוהי.

רבי אברהם הקשיב ברחמים, נשא דברי נחמה ועידוד לנוסע הבעייתי. הוא שיתף סיפורים מהתורה, סיפורי אמונה וחוסן שקיימו את העם היהודי לאורך הדורות.

בחלוף הלילה דיברו רבי אברהם ויוסף עד מאוחר בלילה, קולותיהם מתערבבים ברשרוש העדין של העלים ברוח. וכשהחל אור השחר הראשון להאיר את האופק, הרגיש יוסף תחושת שלווה יורדת עליו, בהירות נפש ולב שלא הכיר מעולם.

בימים שלאחר מכן נשאר יוסף בבית אל, כשהוא ספוג בחכמתו של רבי אברהם ושוקע במסורות הכפר. נחמה מצא במקצבי החיים הפשוטים, ביופיו של הטבע ובחמימות הקהילה שאפפה אותו.

אבל בדיוק כשיוסף התחיל להרגיש בבית בבית אל, היכתה טרגדיה בכפר. בצורת עזה ירדה על הארץ, קמלה יבולים וייבשה את הנחלים שהזינו את שדות הכפר וגני הכפר.

תושבי בית אל הפכו נואשים, קהילתם שפעם משגשגת נאבקת כעת כדי לשרוד מול הרעב והמצוקה. רבי אברהם קרא לתושבי הכפר לפנות אל ה' בתפילה, לבקש את רחמיו והדרכתו בשעת הצורך.

יחדיו התאספו תושבי הכפר בכיכר העיר, לבם כבד מדאגה ופחד. רבי אברהם עמד לפניהם, קולו מצלצל בחגיגיות שציתה את תשומת לבם.

"חברים יקרים", אמר, "עמדנו בפני הרבה נסיונות ותלאות בחיינו, אבל תמיד יצאנו חזקים ועמידים יותר מבעבר. הבה נפנה לאלוהים כעת, בלב עניו ובאמונה איתנה, ונבטח בו שהוא יפרנס אותנו בשעת צרכינו".

עם דמעות בעיניים הרכינו תושבי הכפר את ראשם בתפילה, קולם עולה במקהלה של תחינה ותקווה. ובעודם התפללו, התרחש נס.

מן השמים החלו להתאסף עננים כהים, וגשם עדין החל לרדת על האדמה היבשה. אנשי בית אל הרימו את מבטם ביראת כבוד, לבם מלא תודה ופליאה כשהגשמים המשיכו לזלוג, להזין את הארץ ולהחזיר חיים לכפרם.

בעקבות הבצורת התכנסו אנשי בית אל כפי שלא היו מעולם, מאוחדים באמונתם ותודתם על הברכות שקיבלו. ויוסף, הנוסע העייף שחיפש נחמה בקרבם, מצא לא רק את התשובות שחיפש, אלא תחושת שייכות ומטרה שלא תיאר לעצמו.

ככל שחלפו השנים הפך סיפור בית אל והצלה המופלאה מהבצורת לאגדה, שעברה בדורות כעדות לכוחה של האמונה ולטובת ה'. ורבי אברהם, הזקן החכם שהדריך את עמו בשעתם החשוכה ביותר, נזכר כמגדלור של תקווה והשראה לכל הבאים אחריו.

Translation:

A Miracle in Bethel

Once upon a time, in the ancient land of Israel, there was a village nestled between rolling hills and lush valleys. This village became known as Beit El, and its inhabitants lived a simple but fulfilling life, guided by traditions passed down through the generations.

In Beit El lived a wise old man named Rabbi Avraham. He was revered by everyone in the village for his knowledge of the Torah and his unwavering faith in God. Rabbi Avraham spent his days teaching the young, advising the injured and guiding the needy.

One evening, when Rabbi Avraham was sitting outside his humble abode, looking at the twinkling stars from above, a tired traveler approached him. The traveler's name was Joseph, and he traveled from a distant land in search of answers to life's deep questions.

Yosef explained to Rabbi Avraham that he had heard about the village of Beit El and its renowned sage, and he hoped that the rabbi would be able to offer him the wisdom he requested. Rabbi Avraham welcomed Yosef into his home and listened attentively as the traveler poured out his heart.

Yosef spoke about his struggles and doubts, the trials he faced on his journey and the emptiness he felt inside. He longed to find meaning and purpose in his life, to understand his place in the world and his relationship with the divine.

Rabbi Avraham listened compassionately, offering words of comfort and encouragement to the troubled traveler. He shared stories from the Torah, stories of faith and resilience that sustained the Jewish people throughout the generations.

As the night passed, Rabbi Avraham and Yosef talked until late at night, their voices mixing with the gentle rustling of the leaves in the wind. And when the first light of dawn began to illuminate the horizon, Joseph felt a sense of peace descend upon him, a clarity of mind and heart that he had never known before.

In the days that followed, Yosef remained in Beit El, steeped in Rabbi Avraham's wisdom and immersed in the traditions of the village. He found comfort in the simple rhythms of life, the beauty of nature and the warmth of the community that surrounded him.

But just when Yosef was starting to feel at home in Bethel, tragedy struck the village. A severe drought descended on the land, withered crops and dried up the streams that fed the village fields and gardens.

The residents of Beit El have become desperate, their once thriving community now struggling to survive in the face of hunger and hardship. Rabbi Avraham called the residents of the village to turn to God in prayer, to ask for His mercy and guidance in times of need.

Together the villagers gathered in the city square, their hearts heavy with worry and fear. Rabbi Avraham stood before them, his voice ringing with a solemnity that ignited their attention.

"Dear friends," he said, "we have faced many trials and tribulations in our lives, but we have always come out stronger and more durable than before. Let us turn to God now, with a humble heart and firm faith, and trust in him that he will provide for us in our time of need."

With tears in their eyes, the villagers bowed their heads in prayer, their voices rising in a chorus of supplication and hope. And while they were praying, a miracle happened.

Dark clouds began to gather from the sky, and a gentle rain began to fall on the dry land. The people of Beit El looked up in reverence, their hearts full of gratitude and wonder as the rains continued to pour, nourishing the land and bringing life back to their village.

Following the drought, the people of Beit El gathered like never before, united in their faith and gratitude for the blessings they received. And Yosef, the weary traveler who sought solace among them, found not only the answers he was looking for, but a sense of belonging and a purpose he had never imagined.

As the years passed, the story of Bethel and the miraculous rescue from the drought became a legend, passed down through the generations as a testimony to the power of faith and the goodness of God. And Rabbi Avraham, the wise old man who guided his people in their darkest hour, is remembered as a beacon of hope and inspiration to all who follow him.

4. אגדת האגם מואר הירח

עמוק בלב שממה יהודה, היכן שהשטח הפרוע פוגש את המרחב האינסופי של המדבר, שוכן מקלט נסתר המוכר רק למעטים נבחרים. השוכן בין צוקים נישאים ויערות עתיקים, האגם מואר הירח מנצנץ כמו תכשיט תחת אור הירח המלא, מימיו חדורים בזוהר אתרי השואב את הנשמה.

על פי האגדה המקומית, מקורותיו של האגם מואר הירח ספוג מסתורין וקסם. אומרים שלפני אלפי שנים, כשהעולם עוד היה צעיר והאלים התהלכו בין בני תמותה, בכתה אלילה גדולה דמעות של צער על סבל האנושות. הדמעות הללו, החדורות במהותה האלוהית, נפלו על האדמה ויצרו את מימי האגם השלווים, עדות לחמלה והזדהות של האלה כלפי כל היצורים החיים.

מאז ומתמיד, האגם מואר הירח נערץ כמקום קדוש של ריפוי והתחדשות, שאליו מגיעים מטיילים עייפים ונשמות מוטרדות לחפש נחמה והדרכה בעת צרה. אומרים שהמימיים המיסטיים שלו בעלי הכוח לטהר את הרוח ולהחזיר את האיזון לנפש הבעייתית, ומציעים מקלט מהכאוס והמהומה של העולם שמעבר.

בין תושבי הכפר השוכנים בכפרים ובמשקים הסמוכים, מסופר על עלמה צעירה בשם ליאורה, שגורלה נשזר בגורלו של האגם המואר בדרכים שאיש לא יכול היה לחזות מראש. בעיניה הזוהרות ובחיוכה הזוהר, ליאורה הייתה מגדלור של אור בחושך, החסד והחמלה שלה נוגעים בחייהם של כל מי שחצה את דרכה.

בליל הירח המלא, כשהעולם היה שטוף בזוהר הכסוף של אור הירח, חשה ליאורה משיכה שאי אפשר לעמוד בפניה מושכת אותה לעבר חופי האגם המואר. מונחית על ידי אינטואיציה עתיקה שהתרגשה בנפשה, היא יצאה למסע אל הלא נודע, לבה מלא בתחושת פליאה וציפייה.

כשהתקרבה לשפת האגם, התגברה על ליאורה תחושת יראה מהמראה שלפניה. מי האגם נצצו כמו כסף נוזלי באור הירח, פני השטח שלהם אדוות באנרגיה עולמית שכמו קורצת אליה קרוב יותר. ללא היסוס, היא השתכשכה אל הרדודים, רגליה היחפות שוקעות בבוץ הרך כשהיא מתמסרת לחיבוק האגם.

כשהיא שקעה מתחת לפני השטח, חשה ליאורה תחושת שלווה עמוקה שוטפת אותה, כאילו חזרה הביתה למקום שמעולם לא הכירה. המים עטפו אותה בחיבוק הקריר שלהם, הליטוף העדין שלהם מרגיע את מוחה הטורד ומסיר את העול מלבה העייף.

במעמקי האגם נתקלה ליאורה בעולם שלא דומה לאף אחד שהכירה אי פעם, ממלכה של אור וצל מנצנצים שבו הזמן כאילו עמד מלכת. היא רקדה עם רוחות המים, מסתובבת ומסתובבת בבלט חינני של תנועה ומוזיקה, צחוקה מהדהד דרך מערות המעמקים.

כשהלילה חלף ואור השחר הראשון החל לפרוץ מעבר לאופק, ידעה ליאורה שהזמן שלה באגם מתקרב. בתחושת חוסר רצון היא עלתה מהמים, רוחה השתנתה לנצח בגלל הקסם שחוותה.

מאותו יום ואילך, ליאורה נודעה כשומרת האגם מואר הירח, דמות מיסטית הנערצת על כל מי שחיפש נחמה ומקלט במימיו. נוכחותה הורגשה ברחבי הארץ, רוחה העדינה מנחה ומגנה על הנזקקים, אהבתה לאגם ולמסתורין שלו לעולם לא מתערערת.

ולמרות שהשנים חלפו והעולם השתנה סביבה, ליאורה נשארה איתנה במסירותה לאגם מואר הירח, הקשר שלה עם מימיו בלתי שביר ורוחה שזורה לנצח ביופיו הנצחי. שכן בלב השממה, בין האורנים הלוחשים והצוקים המהדהדים, חיה האגדה על ליאורה ואגם מואר הירח, עדות לכוח המתמשך של קסם, מסתורין ורוח האדם.

Translation:

The Legend of the Moonlit Lake

Deep in the heart of the Judean wilderness, where the rugged terrain meets the endless expanse of the desert, there lies a hidden sanctuary known only to a select few. Nestled amidst towering cliffs and ancient forests, the Moonlit Lake shimmers like a jewel under the light of the full moon, its waters imbued with an ethereal glow that captivates the soul.

According to local legend, the origins of the Moonlit Lake are steeped in mystery and magic. It is said that millennia ago, when the world was still young and the gods walked among mortals, a great goddess wept tears of sorrow for the suffering of humanity. These tears, imbued with her divine essence, fell upon the earth and formed the tranquil waters of the lake, a testament to the goddess's compassion and empathy for all living beings.

Since time immemorial, the Moonlit Lake has been revered as a sacred place of healing and renewal, where weary travelers and troubled souls come to seek solace and guidance in times of need. Its mystical waters are said to possess the power to cleanse the spirit and restore balance to the troubled mind, offering a sanctuary from the chaos and turmoil of the world beyond.

Among the villagers who dwell in the nearby hamlets and homesteads, there is a tale told of a young maiden named Liora, whose fate became intertwined with that of the Moonlit Lake in ways no one could have foreseen. With her luminous eyes and radiant smile, Liora was a beacon of light in the darkness, her kindness and compassion touching the lives of all who crossed her path.

On the night of the full moon, when the world was bathed in the silver glow of lunar light, Liora felt an irresistible pull drawing her towards the shores of the Moonlit Lake. Guided by an ancient intuition that stirred within her soul, she embarked on a journey into the unknown, her heart filled with a sense of wonder and anticipation.

As she approached the edge of the lake, Liora was overcome by a sense of awe at the sight before her. The waters of the lake shimmered like liquid silver in the moonlight, their surface rippling with an otherworldly energy that seemed to beckon her closer. Without hesitation, she waded into the shallows, her bare feet sinking into the soft mud as she surrendered herself to the embrace of the lake.

As she submerged herself beneath the surface, Liora felt a profound sense of peace wash over her, as if she had come home to a place she had never known. The waters enveloped her in their cool embrace, their gentle caress soothing her troubled mind and lifting the burdens from her weary heart.

In the depths of the lake, Liora encountered a world unlike any she had ever known, a realm of shimmering light and shadow where time seemed to stand still. She danced with the spirits of the water, twirling and spinning in a graceful ballet of movement and music, her laughter echoing through the caverns of the deep.

As the night wore on and the first light of dawn began to break across the horizon, Liora knew that her time in the lake was drawing to a close. With a sense of reluctance, she surfaced from the waters, her spirit forever changed by the magic she had experienced.

From that day forward, Liora became known as the Guardian of the Moonlit Lake, a mystical figure revered by all who sought solace and sanctuary in its waters. Her presence was felt throughout the land, her gentle spirit guiding and protecting those in need, her love for the lake and its mysteries never wavering.

And though the years passed and the world changed around her, Liora remained steadfast in her devotion to the Moonlit Lake, her bond with its waters unbreakable and her spirit forever intertwined with its timeless beauty. For in the heart of the wilderness, amidst the whispering pines and the echoing cliffs, the legend of Liora and the Moonlit Lake lived on, a testament to the enduring power of magic, mystery, and the human spirit.

5. מתנת האורג

פעם, בשוק שוקק חיים השוכן בלב עיר תוססת, שכן אורג בשם אבנר. החנות הקטנה שלו, המעוטרת בבריחים של בד צבעוני והצלצול הקצבי של הנול שלו, עמדה כעדות לשליטתו במלאכה. אבנר נודע למרחקים בזכות ידיו המיומנות ובעין החדה לפרטים, תוך שזירת דוגמאות מורכבות ועיצובים תוססים שסנוורו את העיניים ושבו את הדמיון.

למרות כישרונו, אבנר היה איש צנוע, מרוצה לבלות את ימיו בבדידות שקטה, אבוד בקצב עבודתו. אבל עמוק בתוך לבו, בערה תשוקה עזה, כמיהה ליצור משהו באמת יוצא דופן, יצירת מופת שתשאיר חותם בל יימחה על העולם.

יום גורלי אחד, כשאבנר ישב ליד הנול שלו, מוחו מלא בחלומות של גדלות, נכנס זר לחנותו. לבוש בגלימה של ארגמן עמוק ונושא אווירה של מסתורין, הזר הציג את עצמו כאליאס, נוסע מארץ רחוקה. אליאס, מסוקרן מהמוניטין של אבנר, הביע עניין רב בעבודתו של האורג, עיניו נדלקות מסקרנות והערצה.

בהתלהבות לחלוק את מלאכתו עם חבר נלהב, קיבל אבנר את אליאס בחנותו, והזמין אותו להתבונן בזמן עבודתו. ככל שחלפו השעות, השניים החליפו סיפורים וצחוקים, ידידותם פרחה כמו עלי כותרת של פרח בחום השמש.

נרגש מהמסירות והתשוקה של אבנר, אליאס גילה את עצמו כיותר מסתם מטייל. הוא היה שליח שנשלח על ידי האלים עצמם, נושא מתנה של כוח מופלא ופוטנציאל בלתי ידוע. בפריחה, הוא הוציא נרתיק קטן מתוך גלימתו והגיש אותו לאבנר, עיניו נוצצות בציפייה.

בידיים רועדות, אבנר פתח את הנרתיק כדי לחשוף פקעת חוט שלא דומה לשום דבר שראה בעבר. צבעיו נצצו ורקדו באור, טווים שטיח של פליאה וקסם שמילא את ליבו של אבנר ביראה.

"זה לא שרשור רגיל", הסביר אליאס. "זו מתנה מהאלים, שניתנה למי שליבם טהור וידיהם מיומנות. בחוט זה יש לך את הכוח ליצור יצירות אמנות שידהימו ויעוררו השראה בכל מי שמתבונן בהן".

מוצף תודה ותמיהה קיבל אבנר את המתנה, מוחו רוחש מהתרגשות ואפשרות. בעידודו של אליאס, הוא התחיל לעבוד מיד, אצבעותיו עפות על הנול כשהוא טווה את החוט לתוך הבד המעודן ביותר שיצר אי פעם.

ימים הפכו לשבועות, ושבועות הפכו לחודשים, כשאבנר שפך את לבו ונשמתו ביצירתו, ויצר שטיחי יופי ומורכבות שאין שני להם. כל יצירה הייתה עוצרת נשימה מהקודמת, משכה אליה מעריצים ופטרונים מרחוק ומרחוק שהתפעלו מפלא האמנות שלו.

אבל ככל שחלף הזמן, אבנר החל להבין שהערך האמיתי של מתנתו טמון לא ביופיים של יצירותיו, אלא בשמחה ובפליאה שהביאו לאחרים. בהשראת טוב הלב והנדיבות של אליאס, הוא החליט להשתמש בכישרון שלו לא למען תהילה או עושר, אלא למען שיפור הקהילה שלו והעולם הסובב אותו.

וכך, בכל חוט ששזר ובכל דוגמה שעיצב, ביקש אבנר להפיץ אהבה ויופי לכל מי שחצה את דרכו, לבו אסיר תודה לנצח על מתנת האלים ועל ידידותו של זר בשם אליאס.

"מתנת האורג" הפכה לאגדה בעיר, עדות לכוחה של טוב לב, יצירתיות, והקסם הטרנספורמטיבי של הידידות. ולמרות שבסופו של דבר ידיו של אבנר הזדקנו והנול שלו השתתק, מורשתו חיה בלבם ובמוחם של כל מי שהכיר אותו, דוגמה נוצצת לדברים יוצאי הדופן שניתן להשיג כאשר אדם הולך בעקבות התשוקה שלהם ומאמץ את המתנות שיש להם ניתן.

Translation:

The Weaver's Gift

Once upon a time, in a bustling marketplace nestled within the heart of a vibrant city, there dwelled a weaver named Avner. His small shop, adorned with bolts of colorful fabric and the rhythmic clacking of his loom, stood as a testament to his mastery of the craft. Avner was known far and wide for his skillful hands and keen eye for detail, weaving intricate patterns and vibrant designs that dazzled the eyes and captured the imagination.

Despite his talent, Avner was a humble man, content to spend his days in quiet solitude, lost in the rhythm of his work. But deep within his heart, there burned a fierce passion, a yearning to create something truly extraordinary, a masterpiece that would leave an indelible mark upon the world.

One fateful day, as Avner sat at his loom, his mind filled with dreams of greatness, a stranger entered his shop. Clad in a cloak of deep crimson and bearing an air of mystery, the stranger introduced himself as Elias, a traveler from a distant land. Intrigued by Avner's reputation, Elias expressed a keen interest in the weaver's work, his eyes alight with curiosity and admiration.

Eager to share his craft with a fellow enthusiast, Avner welcomed Elias into his shop, inviting him to observe as he worked. As the hours passed, the two men exchanged stories and laughter, their friendship blossoming like the petals of a flower in the warmth of the sun.

Moved by Avner's dedication and passion, Elias revealed himself to be more than just a traveler. He was a messenger sent by the gods themselves, bearing a gift of wondrous power and untold potential. With a flourish, he produced a small pouch from within his cloak and presented it to Avner, his eyes sparkling with anticipation.

With trembling hands, Avner opened the pouch to reveal a skein of thread unlike any he had ever seen before. Its colors shimmered and danced in the light, weaving a tapestry of wonder and enchantment that filled Avner's heart with awe.

"This is no ordinary thread," Elias explained. "It is a gift from the gods, bestowed upon those whose hearts are pure and whose hands are skilled. With this thread, you have the power to create works of art that will astonish and inspire all who behold them."

Overwhelmed with gratitude and wonder, Avner accepted the gift, his mind buzzing with excitement and possibility. With Elias's encouragement, he set to work immediately, his fingers flying across the loom as he wove the thread into the most exquisite fabric he had ever created.

Days turned into weeks, and weeks turned into months, as Avner poured his heart and soul into his work, creating tapestries of unparalleled beauty and complexity. Each piece was more breathtaking than the last, drawing admirers and patrons from far and wide who marveled at the wonder of his art.

But as time passed, Avner began to realize that the true value of his gift lay not in the beauty of his creations, but in the joy and wonder they brought to others. Inspired by Elias's kindness and generosity, he resolved to use his talent not for fame or fortune, but for the betterment of his community and the world around him.

And so, with each thread he wove and each pattern he designed, Avner sought to spread love and beauty to all who crossed his path, his heart forever grateful for the gift of the gods and the friendship of a stranger named Elias.

"The Weaver's Gift" became a legend in the city, a testament to the power of kindness, creativity, and the transformative magic of friendship. And though Avner's hands eventually grew old and his loom fell silent, his legacy lived on in the hearts and minds of all who knew him, a shining example of the extraordinary things that can be achieved when one follows their passion and embraces the gifts they have been given.

6. סיפורו של איתן והיער הקסום

פעם, בממלכת אנקריה, שבה הרים נישאים נישקו לשמיים ויערות אזמרגד נמתחים ככל שהעין יכולה לראות, חי בחור צעיר בשם איתן. איתן, שנולד תחת אור הירח הכסוף, מבורך על ידי רוחות הארץ העתיקות, נועד לגדולה מהרגע שהוא נשף את נשימתו הראשונה.

מגיל צעיר גילה איתן סקרנות חסרת גבול וצימאון בלתי נדלה להרפתקאות. בזמן שילדים אחרים שיחקו בבטחון הכפר שלהם, איתן היה משוטט במעמקי היער, לבו חי עם הבטחה לגילוי.

ככל שהתבגר, תאוות הנדודים של איתן רק התגברה, והניעה אותו לחקור כל פינה בממלכה ולחפש את הפלאים הנסתרים שנמצאים מעבר לגבולותיה. עם כל מסע חדש, הוא התחזק, חכם יותר והתכוונן יותר למקצבים של עולם הטבע.

יום גורלי אחד, כשאיתן שוטט בפאתי הכפר שלו, הוא נקלע לשביל נסתר המוביל עמוק ללב היער. מסוקרן מהתעלומות שמעבר, הוא עקב אחרי השביל המתפתל, חושיו חיים בציפייה.

ככל שהעמיק לתוך היער, איתן מצא את עצמו מוקף בעצים נישאים ובעלווה עבותה, האוויר עבה בניחוח מתוק של פרחי בר וקריאות רחוקות של יצורי החורש. הוא הרגיש תחושת פליאה ויראה שוטפת אותו, כאילו נכנס לעולם שהזמן לא נגע בו.

אבל כשהשמש התחילה לשקוע והצללים התארכו, איתן הבין שהוא אבוד. בהלה אחזה בלבו כשחיפש בטירוף אחר דרך לצאת מהיער, אבל החופה הצפופה מעליו הסתירה את הכוכבים והשאירה אותו מבולבל.

בדיוק כשכל התקווה נראתה אבודה, איתן נתקל בקרחת יער שטופת אור ירח, במרכזה נשלט עץ מרהיב שלא דומה לאף עץ שראה עד כה. ענפיו נמתחו גבוה אל שמי הלילה, העלים שלו מנצנצים בזוהר של עולם אחר.

נמשך בדחף שאי אפשר לעמוד בפניו, איתן ניגש אל העץ והושיט יד לגעת בגזע שלו. לתדהמתו, הקליפה הרגישה חמימה וחיה מתחת לקצות אצבעותיו, פועמת באנרגיה שנראתה מהדהדת עמוק בתוך נשמתו.

כשהוא עמד מתחת לעץ, קול הדהד מבעד לבהיר, עדין אך עוצמתי, ממלא את מוחו של איתן בחזיונות העבר ובנבואות העתיד. הוא דיבר על קסם עתיק ואוצרות נסתרים, על ניסיונות ותלאות שיבחנו את אומץ ליבו ואת נחישותו.

נחוש בדעתו לחשוף את סודות היער הקסום ולהוכיח שהוא ראוי למתנותיו, יצא איתן למסע שיוביל אותו למקומות הרחוקים ביותר של הממלכה ומחוצה לה. בדרך, הוא נתקל ביצורים מסתוריים והתמודד עם אתגרים אדירים, כל אחד מקרב אותו אל האמת שחיפש.

דרך יערות אפלים והרים בוגדניים, על פני מדבריות עצומות וימים סוערים, המשיך איתן, נחישותו בלתי מעורערת גם מול סיכויים בלתי עבירים לכאורה. עם כל צעד שצעד, הוא התחזק והחכים, רוחו התמתן על ידי ניסיונות מסעו.

וכאשר עמד לבסוף מול לב היער המכושף, ידע שגורלו מצפה לו. בלב מלא אומץ ורוח בוערת בנחישות, צעד איתן אל הלא נודע, מוכן לחבק את כל ההרפתקאות שצפויות לו.

"סיפור איתן והיער המכושף" הפך לאגדה בממלכה, עדות לעוצמת הסקרנות, האומץ והרוח האנושית הבלתי ניתנת לשליטה. ולמרות שפרטי מסעו של איתן אבדו לזמן, שמו התקיים בליבם ובמוחם של כל מי ששמע את סיפורו, תזכורת לכך שההרפתקאות הגדולות ביותר הן אלו שמתחילות בצעד אחד אל הלא נודע.

Translation:

The Tale of Eitan and the Enchanted Forest

Once upon a time, in the realm of Ancaria, where towering mountains kissed the sky and emerald forests stretched as far as the eye could see, there lived a young man named Eitan. Born under the silver moonlight and blessed by the ancient spirits of the land, Eitan was destined for greatness from the moment he drew his first breath.

From an early age, Eitan displayed a boundless curiosity and an insatiable thirst for adventure. While other children played in the safety of their village, Eitan would wander into the depths of the forest, his heart alive with the promise of discovery.

As he grew older, Eitan's wanderlust only intensified, driving him to explore every corner of the kingdom and seek out the hidden wonders that lay beyond its borders. With each new journey, he grew stronger, wiser, and more attuned to the rhythms of the natural world.

One fateful day, as Eitan roamed the outskirts of his village, he stumbled upon a hidden path leading deep into the heart of the forest. Intrigued by the mysteries that lay beyond, he followed the winding trail, his senses alive with anticipation.

As he ventured deeper into the forest, Eitan found himself surrounded by towering trees and lush foliage, the air thick with the sweet scent of wildflowers and the distant calls of woodland creatures. He felt a sense of wonder and awe wash over him, as if he had stepped into a world untouched by time.

But as the sun began to set and the shadows grew long, Eitan realized that he was lost. Panic seized his heart as he searched frantically for a way out of the forest, but the dense canopy overhead obscured the stars and left him disoriented.

Just when all hope seemed lost, Eitan stumbled upon a clearing bathed in moonlight, its center dominated by a magnificent tree unlike any he had ever seen before. Its branches stretched high into the night sky, its leaves shimmering with an otherworldly glow.

Drawn by an irresistible impulse, Eitan approached the tree and reached out to touch its trunk. To his astonishment, the bark felt warm and alive beneath his fingertips, pulsing with an energy that seemed to resonate deep within his soul.

As he stood beneath the tree, a voice echoed through the clearing, gentle yet powerful, filling Eitan's mind with visions of the past and prophecies of the future. It spoke of ancient magic and hidden treasures, of trials and tribulations that would test his courage and resolve.

Determined to uncover the secrets of the enchanted forest and prove himself worthy of its gifts, Eitan embarked on a quest that would take him to the farthest reaches of the kingdom and beyond.

Along the way, he encountered mysterious beings and faced formidable challenges, each one bringing him closer to the truth he sought.

Through dark forests and treacherous mountains, across vast deserts and stormy seas, Eitan pressed on, his determination unwavering even in the face of seemingly insurmountable odds. With each step he took, he grew stronger and wiser, his spirit tempered by the trials of his journey.

And when at last he stood before the heart of the enchanted forest, he knew that his destiny awaited him. With a heart full of courage and a spirit aflame with determination, Eitan stepped into the unknown, ready to embrace whatever adventures lay ahead.

"The Tale of Eitan and the Enchanted Forest" became a legend in the kingdom, a testament to the power of curiosity, courage, and the indomitable human spirit. And though the details of Eitan's journey were lost to time, his name lived on in the hearts and minds of all who heard his story, a reminder that the greatest adventures are those that begin with a single step into the unknown.

7. הקמיע האבוד של אלארה

בממלכת אלרה העתיקה, שבה ההרים המכוסים בערפל נשקו לשמים והיערות לחשו סודות של פעם, הייתה אגדה עתיקה כמו הזמן עצמו - אגדה על חפץ רב עוצמה המכונה קמיע השליטה באלמנטים. במשך מאות שנים, הקמיע הקסום הזה הועבר דרך השושלת המלכותית, כוחו האמיתי ידוע רק למעטים הנבחרים שנשאו את משקלו על ליבם.

מוגן בכישופים רבי עוצמה וחבוי עמוק בתוך מסדרונות המבוך של ארמון המלוכה, הקמיע שימש סמל לשגשוג הממלכה ומקור כוח בעת צרה. בעזרת הקסם שלו, שליטי אלרה יכלו לשלוט באלמנטים עצמם, לכופף רוח ומים, אש ואדמה לרצונם.

אך ככל שחלפו מאות השנים וזיכרון כוחו האמיתי של הקמיע התפוגג לאגדה, החלו להתפשט לחישות של אלה שביקשו לתבוע את כוחו בעצמם. ביניהם היה מלאכי, מכשף בעל שם אפל שתאוות הכוח שלו לא ידעה גבול.

מונע על ידי צימאון לשליטה על אלמנטים ומתודלק על ידי לחישות של נבואות עתיקות, מלאכי רקם מזימה מרושעת לתפוס את הקמיע ולכופף את כוחו למטרות האפלות שלו. הוא אסף חבורה של שכירי חרב חסרי רחמים ומכשפים אפלים לצדו, הוא שם את עיניו על ממלכת אלארה, נחוש לתבוע את הקמע כשלו.

בחסות החושך, מלאכי וחניכיו פתחו בפשיטה נועזת על ארמון המלוכה, כשהקסם האפל שלהם קורע את הגנות הממלכה כמו להב דרך משי. למרות מאמציו האמיץ של המשמר המלכותי, הם לא עמדו בכוחו האפל של המכשף, ובזה אחר זה הם נפלו לפני הסתערותו.

עם הארמון כאוס ומשפחת המלוכה בסכנה, התקווה נראתה אבודה לממלכת אלארה. אבל בתוך הכאוס, צץ שביב של תקווה - הרפתקן צעיר בשם קיאלה, שלאומץ הלב והנחישות שלו לא ידעו גבול.

קיאלה, שנולדה ממוצא צנוע אך בורכה ברוח עזה כמו להבת הדרקון, חלמה זמן רב לצאת להרפתקה גדולה כדי להוכיח שהיא ראויה לאגדות ששמעה מאז ילדותה. ועכשיו, כשהחושך איים לבלוע את הממלכה, היא ראתה את ההזדמנות להטביע את חותמה על העולם.

קאילה, שאספה את האומץ והשכל שלה, יצאה למסע מסוכן כדי להחזיר את הקמיע האבוד ולהחזיר את השקט לממלכה. עם חבריה הנאמנים לצידה - קשת מיומן בשם רורן, חכם חכם בשם ליירה ולוחם חסר פחד בשם ת'ורן - היא העזה אל לב היער, שם אורבים צללים אפלים ורעות עתיקות מתחוללות.

מסעם היה רווי סכנה בכל צעד ושעל, כשהם התמודדו עם שטח בוגדני, מלכודות קטלניות ויצורים אכזריים שביקשו לסכל את התקדמותם בכל צעד. אבל עם כל מכשול שהם התגברו, הקשר ביניהם התחזק, נחישותם איתנה, עד ששום דבר לא יכול היה לעמוד בדרכם.

לבסוף, לאחר שבועות רבים של נסיעות, הם הגיעו למצודה החשוכה בו שכבו מלאכי וחניכיו. בהתגנבות ובערמומיות הם חדרו למצודה בחסות הלילה, נחושים להתעמת עם המכשף ולתבוע בחזרה את הקמיע הגנוב.

אבל כשהם התעמקו בלב המבצה, הם נתקלו במלכודות ובמכשולים שנועדו לסכל את התקדמותם, כל אחד ערמומי וקטלני יותר מקודמו. עם זאת, אומץ ליבו וכושר ההמצאה של קאלה גברו, ולבסוף, הם הגיעו לקודש הקודש הפנימי שבו חיכה מלאכי, הקמיע הגנוב נאחז באחיזתו.

קרב עז התפתח, כשקאילה וחברותיה נלחמו בגבורה נגד מלאכי והקסם האפל שלו. לחשים עפו כמו ברק, והאדמה ממש רעדה מתחת לרגליהם כשהם התנגשו בכל כוחם. אבל בסופו של דבר, הנחישות הבלתי מעורערת של קאלה והכוח של חבריה היו אלה שנשאו את היום.

עם גל עוצמה אחרון ונואש, קאלה שלפה את הקמע מאחיזתו של מלאכי, האנרגיות העתיקות שלו מתפצחות סביבה כשהיא החזיקה אותו למעלה. באותו רגע, השמים מעל אלרה התבהרו, והשמש פרצה מבעד לעננים, והטילה שוב את אור הזהב שלה על הממלכה.

בזמן שאנשי אלארה שמחו וחגגו את חירותם החדשה, קיאלה וחברותיה ניצחו, משימתם התמלאה ושמותיהם חרוטים לנצח בדברי ימי ההיסטוריה. ואף על פי שהמסע שלהם היה מסוכן ועתיר סכנה, הם ידעו שקשרי הידידות וכוח התקווה ידריכו אותם בכל האתגרים שעומדים לפניהם.

"הקמיע האבוד של אלארה" הפך לאגדה בממלכה, עדות לרוחם הבלתי ניתנת לשליטה של מי שמעיז לעמוד מול כוחות האופל ולהילחם על מה שנכון. ולמרות שהסיפור יסופר לדורות הבאים, הוא תמיד ייזכר כתזכורת לכך שגם בזמנים האפלים ביותר, התקווה זורחת יותר מכל.

Translation:

The Lost Amulet of Elara

In the ancient kingdom of Elara, where the mist-covered mountains kissed the sky and the forests whispered secrets of old, there existed a legend as old as time itself—a legend of a powerful artifact known as the Amulet of Elemental Mastery. For centuries, this enchanted amulet had been passed down through the royal lineage, its true power known only to the chosen few who bore its weight upon their hearts.

Protected by powerful enchantments and hidden deep within the labyrinthine corridors of the royal palace, the amulet served as a symbol of the kingdom's prosperity and a source of strength in times of need. With its magic, the rulers of Elara could control the elements themselves, bending wind and water, fire and earth to their will.

But as the centuries passed and the memory of the amulet's true power faded into legend, whispers began to spread of those who sought to claim its power for themselves. Among them was Malachi, a sorcerer of dark renown whose lust for power knew no bounds.

Driven by a thirst for dominion over the elements and fueled by the whispers of ancient prophecies, Malachi hatched a nefarious plot to seize the amulet and bend its power to his own dark purposes. Gathering a band of ruthless mercenaries and dark mages to his side, he set his sights on the kingdom of Elara, determined to claim the amulet as his own.

Under the cover of darkness, Malachi and his minions launched a daring raid on the royal palace, their dark magic tearing through the defenses of the kingdom like a blade through silk. Despite the valiant efforts of the royal guard, they were no match for the sorcerer's dark power, and one by one, they fell before his onslaught.

With the palace in chaos and the royal family in peril, hope seemed lost for the kingdom of Elara. But amidst the chaos, a glimmer of hope emerged—a young adventurer named Kaela, whose courage and determination knew no bounds.

Born of humble origins but blessed with a spirit as fierce as the dragon's flame, Kaela had long dreamed of embarking on a grand adventure to prove herself worthy of the legends she had heard since childhood. And now, as darkness threatened to engulf the kingdom, she saw her chance to make her mark upon the world.

Gathering her courage and her wits, Kaela set out on a perilous journey to reclaim the lost amulet and restore peace to the kingdom. With her loyal companions by her side—a skilled archer named Roran, a wise sage named Lyra, and a fearless warrior named Thorne—she ventured into the heart of the forest, where dark shadows lurked and ancient evils stirred.

Their journey was fraught with danger at every turn, as they faced treacherous terrain, deadly traps, and fierce creatures that sought to thwart their progress at every step. But with each obstacle they overcame, their bond grew stronger, their resolve firmer, until nothing could stand in their way.

At last, after many weeks of travel, they arrived at the dark fortress where Malachi and his minions lay in wait. With stealth and cunning, they infiltrated the fortress under cover of night, determined to confront the sorcerer and reclaim the stolen amulet.

But as they delved deeper into the heart of the fortress, they encountered traps and obstacles designed to thwart their progress, each more cunning and deadly than the last. Yet Kaela's courage and ingenuity prevailed, and at last, they reached the inner sanctum where Malachi awaited, the stolen amulet clutched in his grasp.

A fierce battle ensued, as Kaela and her companions fought valiantly against Malachi and his dark magic. Spells flew like lightning, and the very earth trembled beneath their feet as they clashed with all their might. But in the end, it was Kaela's unwavering determination and the strength of her companions that carried the day.

With a final, desperate surge of power, Kaela wrested the amulet from Malachi's grasp, its ancient energies crackling around her as she held it aloft. In that moment, the skies above Elara cleared, and the sun broke through the clouds, casting its golden light upon the kingdom once more.

As the people of Elara rejoiced and celebrated their newfound freedom, Kaela and her companions stood victorious, their quest fulfilled and their names forever etched in the annals of history. And though their journey had been perilous and fraught with danger, they knew that the bonds of friendship and the power of hope would guide them through whatever challenges lay ahead.

"The Lost Amulet of Elara" became a legend in the kingdom, a testament to the indomitable spirit of those who dare to stand against the forces of darkness and fight for what is right. And though the story would be told for generations to come, it would always be remembered as a reminder that even in the darkest of times, hope shines brightest of all.

8. המנגינה של לב הדרקון

בארץ רחוקה, שבה הרים ערפיליים התנשאו גבוה מעל העננים ויערות עתיקים לחשו סודות של פעם, חי פייטן צעיר בשם אריאלה. עם שיער כהה כחצות ועיניים בהירות כמו הכוכבים, לאריאלה הייתה מתנה שהבדילה אותה מכל האחרים - היכולת לשמוע את שירי העולם סביבה.

מהרשרוש העדין של עלים ברוח ועד להתרסקות הגלים הרועמת על החוף, שמעה אריאלה מוזיקה בכל דבר, וטווה מנגינות של פליאה וקסם עם כל תנופה של הלוטה שלה. אבל מכל השירים ששמעה, היה אחד ששבה את לבה מאין כמוהו - המנגינה הרודפת של שירת הדרקון.

במשך מאות שנים שלט הדרקון על הארץ עם טופר ברזל ולב אבן, נשימתו הלוהטת השמידה כפרים ויערות כאחד. אבל בתוך ההרס, היה יופי שאפשר למצוא - יופי בשירת הדרקון, מנגינה רודפת שהדהדה בעמקים ורקדה על הרוח.

מונעת מרצון להבין את סודות שירו של הדרקון, יצאה אריאלה למסע מסוכן למצוא את היצור שכבש את ליבה. עם הלוטה בידה ולב מלא אומץ, היא יצאה אל לב השממה, שם סכנה אורבה בכל פינה וצללים רקדו לאור הירח.

תוך כדי נסיעה, אריאלה נתקלה באתגרים ומכשולים רבים, משטח בוגדני ועד ליצורים אכזריים שביקשו לסכל את התקדמותה. אבל עם כל ניסיון שעמד בפניה, נחישותה רק הלכה והתחזקה, ניזונה מהידיעה ששיר הדרקון מחכה לה בסוף דרכה.

לבסוף, לאחר ימים רבים של מסע, הגיעה אריאלה למאורת הדרקון - מערה של חושך וייאוש, שבה שכב היצור ועיניו בוערות בעוצמה עזה. לא נרתעה מנוכחותה האדירה של החיה, אריאלה התקרבה, הלוטה שלה מורם וקולה יציב.

באצבעות רועדות החלה לנגן - מנגינה של תקווה וגעגוע, של שמחה וצער, שזורה יחד בחוטי לבה. וכשהפתקים מילאו את המערה, קרה משהו מופלא - עיניו של הדרקון התרככו, הבעת פניו עברה מאחת של זעם לזו של סקרנות.

באותו רגע, אריאלה ידעה שהגיעה ללב הדרקון, שמתחת לחיצוניותו המפחידה מסתתרת נשמה המשתוקקת שיבינו אותה. וכך היא ניגנה, שפכה את לבה ונפשה לתוך המוזיקה, עד שלבסוף הדרקון הרים את ראשו והתחיל לשיר.

הצליל לא היה דומה לשום דבר שאריאלה שמעה אי פעם - סימפוניה של כוח וחן, של כוח ופגיעות, שהדהדה דרך המערה ומעבר לה. וכששיר הדרקון מילא את האוויר, הרגישה אריאלה תחושת שלווה עמוקה שוטפת אותה, כאילו סוף סוף מצאה את התשובה שחיפשה כל הזמן.

מאותו יום ואילך, אריאלה והדרקון הפכו לבני לוויה לא סבירים, טיילו יחד בארץ וחלקו את המוזיקה שלהם עם כל מי שהיה מקשיב. ולמרות שהמסע שלהם היה רווי סכנה ואי ודאות, הם ידעו שכל עוד יש להם זה את זה, הם תמיד ימצאו את דרכם הביתה.

"שיר הדרקון" הפך לאגדה בארץ, עדות לכוחה של המוזיקה לגשר על הפער אפילו בין בני לוויה הכי לא סבירים. ולמרות שפרטי המסע של אריאלה אבדו לזמן, שמה חי בלבם ובמוחם של כל מי ששמע את סיפורה, תזכורת שלפעמים, השירים היפים ביותר הם אלה שבאים מהלב.

Translation:

The Melody of the Dragon's Heart

In a distant land, where misty mountains soared high above the clouds and ancient forests whispered secrets of old, there lived a young bard named Ariella. With hair as dark as midnight and eyes as bright as the stars, Ariella possessed a gift that set her apart from all others—the ability to hear the songs of the world around her.

From the gentle rustle of leaves in the wind to the thunderous crash of waves upon the shore, Ariella heard music in everything, weaving melodies of wonder and enchantment with each strum of her lute. But of all the songs she heard, there was one that captivated her heart like no other—the haunting melody of the dragon's song.

For centuries, the dragon had ruled over the land with an iron claw and a heart of stone, its fiery breath laying waste to villages and forests alike. But amidst the destruction, there was a beauty to be found—a beauty in the dragon's song, a haunting melody that echoed through the valleys and danced upon the wind.

Driven by a desire to understand the secrets of the dragon's song, Ariella set out on a perilous journey to find the creature that had captured her heart. With her lute in hand and a heart full of courage, she ventured into the heart of the wilderness, where danger lurked around every corner and shadows danced in the moonlight.

As she traveled, Ariella encountered many challenges and obstacles, from treacherous terrain to fierce creatures that sought to thwart her progress. But with each trial she faced, her resolve only grew stronger, fueled by the knowledge that the dragon's song awaited her at the end of her journey.

At last, after many days of travel, Ariella arrived at the dragon's lair—a cavern of darkness and despair, where the creature lay in wait, its eyes burning with a fierce intensity. Undeterred by the beast's formidable presence, Ariella approached, her lute held high and her voice steady.

With trembling fingers, she began to play—a melody of hope and longing, of joy and sorrow, woven together with the threads of her heart. And as the notes filled the cavern, something miraculous happened—the dragon's eyes softened, its expression shifting from one of rage to one of curiosity.

In that moment, Ariella knew that she had reached the heart of the dragon, that beneath its fearsome exterior lay a soul yearning to be understood. And so she played on, pouring her heart and soul into the music, until at last the dragon lifted its head and began to sing.

The sound was unlike anything Ariella had ever heard before—a symphony of power and grace, of strength and vulnerability, that echoed through the cavern and beyond. And as the dragon's song filled the air, Ariella felt a deep sense of peace wash over her, as if she had finally found the answer she had been seeking all along.

From that day forward, Ariella and the dragon became unlikely companions, traveling the land together and sharing their music with all who would listen. And though their journey was fraught with danger and uncertainty, they knew that as long as they had each other, they would always find their way home.

"The Dragon's Song" became a legend in the land, a testament to the power of music to bridge the gap between even the most unlikely of companions. And though the details of Ariella's journey were lost to time, her name lived on in the hearts and minds of all who heard her story, a reminder that sometimes, the most beautiful songs are the ones that come from the heart.

9. שומר הממלכה הנשכחת

בממלכה עטופה בערפל ומסתורין, שבה היו חורבות עתיקות חבויות מתחת לעלווה הצפופה של היער הקסום, חיה יתומה צעירה בשם ליאורה. נטושה בלידתה וגדלה על ידי החכם הזקן והחכם, עמוס, הייתה ליאורה רוח פראית כמו היער עצמו ולב טהור כטל הבוקר.

מהרגע שיכלה ללכת, ליאורה הייתה משוטטת בשבילי היער, רגליה היחפות רוקדות על האבנים המכוסות אזוב כשהיא רודפת אחרי לחישות הרוח. היא הכירה כל עץ, כל נחל, כל קרחת גג נסתרת, וחשה קרבה עם היצורים שקראו ליער בית.

אבל כשליאורה התבגרה, היא החלה לחוש בחושך אורב בשולי היער - חושך שלחש על סיפורים נשכחים וסודות עתיקים שקבורים זה מכבר מתחת לאדמה. נחושה בדעתה לחשוף את האמת, ליאורה יצאה למסע כדי לפענח את מסתורי היער הקסום ולגלות את ייעודה האמיתי.

מונחית על ידי חוכמתו של עמוס ומתודלקת על ידי הנחישות העזה שלה, ליאורה נסעה עמוק אל לב היער, שם רקדו צללים והדהוד סודות לחשו של פעם. בדרך, היא נתקלה ביצורים מוזרים ומופלאים - ספר שובב שרקד על הבריזה, ינשוף זקן וחכם ששמר על סודות הלילה, ופאון עדין שדיבר בחידות ובחרוזים.

עם כל מפגש, הנחישות של ליאורה רק התחזקה, רוחה לא נרתעה מהאתגרים שצפויים לה. היא התמודדה עם ניסיונות של אש ומים, אדמה ואוויר, כשהיא משתמשת בשנינותה ואומץ ליבה כדי להתגבר על כל מכשול בדרכה. ואף על פי שהמסע היה ארוך ומסוכן, היא ידעה שהיא לא לבד, כי היער עצמו כאילו מנחה את צעדיה ומגן עליה מפגיעה.

לבסוף, לאחר ימים רבים של נסיעות, הגיעה ליאורה ללב היער הקסום - מקום של עוצמה עתיקה וסודות בלתי סופרים, בו המה האוויר באנרגיה של עידנים עברו. שם היא מצאה את מקור החושך שפקד את חלומותיה - ממלכה נשכחת החבויה עמוק מתחת לאדמה, הכניסה אליו נשמרת על ידי יצור מפחיד של אגדה.

בלי להירתע ממראהו העזה של היצור, התקרבה ליאורה, לבה מלא בנחישות ומוחה צלול כשמי הבוקר. ביד יציבה ובקול מלא נחישות, היא דיברה מילים של שלום והבנה, והושיטה יד אל היצור בחסד ובחמלה.

להפתעתה, היצור הגיב בעין יפה, עיניו התרככו כשראה את הילדה הצעירה שלפניו. היא דיברה על חובתה לשמור על הממלכה הנשכחת, לשמור על סודותיה מפני אלה שיבקשו לנצל את כוחה לרווחתם. אבל הוא גם דיבר על הבדידות שפקדה אותו במשך מאות שנים, על הכמיהה לזוגיות ולהבנה.

נגעה ממצבו של היצור, ליאורה הציעה ידידות, והבטיחה לבקר בממלכה הנשכחת וללמוד את סודותיו, אך רק בברכת היצור. וכך, בהנהון ראשו ובהינף זנבו, היצור העניק לה את המעבר, ופתח את הדרך לעולם של פלאים מעבר לדמיון.

יחד, ליאורה והיצור חקרו את הממלכה הנשכחת, חושפים את מסתוריו וחושפים את סודותיו בזה אחר זה. הם נתקלו בשומרים עתיקים ובחפצים רבי עוצמה, כל אחד מחזיק חלק מההיסטוריה של הממלכה ורמז למטרה האמיתית שלו.

וכשהם נסעו עמוק יותר אל לב הממלכה הנשכחת, למדה ליאורה את ייעודה האמיתי - להיות השומר של היער הקסום, להגן על סודותיו ואוצרותיו לכל עת. עם היצור לצידה וחוכמת היער כמורה, היא ידעה שלעולם לא תהיה לבד, כי מצאה את ביתה האמיתי בין העצים והצללים, הלחישות והחלומות.

"שומר הממלכה הנשכחת" הפך לאגדה בממלכה, סיפור על אומץ וחמלה, על ידידות והבנה. ולמרות שפרטי מסעה של ליאורה אבדו לזמן, שמה התקיים בליבם ובמוחם של כל מי ששמע את סיפורה, תזכורת שלפעמים, ההרפתקאות הגדולות ביותר הן אלו שאנו מוצאים כאשר אנו הכי פחות מצפים להן.

Translation:

The Guardian of the Forgotten Realm

In a kingdom shrouded in mist and mystery, where ancient ruins lay hidden beneath the dense foliage of the Enchanted Forest, there lived a young orphan named Liora. Abandoned at birth and raised by the wise old sage, Amos, Liora possessed a spirit as wild as the forest itself and a heart as pure as the morning dew.

From the moment she could walk, Liora would wander the forest trails, her bare feet dancing upon the moss-covered stones as she chased after the whispers of the wind. She knew every tree, every stream, every hidden glade, and felt a kinship with the creatures that called the forest home.

But as Liora grew older, she began to sense a darkness lurking at the edges of the forest—a darkness that whispered of forgotten tales and ancient secrets long buried beneath the earth. Determined to uncover the truth, Liora set out on a quest to unravel the mysteries of the Enchanted Forest and discover her true destiny.

Guided by the wisdom of Amos and fueled by her own fierce determination, Liora journeyed deep into the heart of the forest, where shadows danced and echoes whispered secrets of old. Along the way, she encountered strange and wondrous beings—a mischievous sprite who danced upon the breeze, a wise old owl who guarded the secrets of the night, and a gentle faun who spoke in riddles and rhymes.

With each encounter, Liora's resolve only grew stronger, her spirit undaunted by the challenges that lay ahead. She faced trials of fire and water, earth and air, using her wit and her courage to overcome each obstacle in her path. And though the journey was long and perilous, she knew that she was not alone, for the forest itself seemed to guide her steps and protect her from harm.

At last, after many days of travel, Liora arrived at the heart of the Enchanted Forest—a place of ancient power and untold secrets, where the air hummed with the energy of ages past. There, she found the source of the darkness that had plagued her dreams—a forgotten realm hidden deep beneath the earth, its entrance guarded by a fearsome creature of legend.

Undeterred by the creature's fierce visage, Liora approached, her heart filled with determination and her mind clear as the morning sky. With a steady hand and a voice filled with resolve, she spoke words of peace and understanding, reaching out to the creature with kindness and compassion.

To her surprise, the creature responded in kind, its eyes softening as it beheld the young girl before it. It spoke of its duty to guard the forgotten realm, to keep its secrets safe from those who would seek to exploit its power for their own gain. But it also spoke of the loneliness that had plagued it for centuries, of the longing for companionship and understanding.

Touched by the creature's plight, Liora offered her friendship, promising to visit the forgotten realm and learn its secrets, but only with the creature's blessing. And so, with a nod of its head and a flick of its tail, the creature granted her passage, opening the way to a world of wonders beyond imagining.

Together, Liora and the creature explored the forgotten realm, uncovering its mysteries and unlocking its secrets one by one. They encountered ancient guardians and powerful artifacts, each one holding a piece of the realm's history and a clue to its true purpose.

And as they journeyed deeper into the heart of the forgotten realm, Liora came to understand her true destiny—to be the guardian of the Enchanted Forest, to protect its secrets and its treasures for all time. With the creature by her side and the wisdom of the forest as her guide, she knew that she would never be alone, for she had found her true home among the trees and the shadows, the whispers and the dreams.

"The Guardian of the Forgotten Realm" became a legend in the kingdom, a tale of courage and compassion, of friendship and understanding. And though the details of Liora's journey were lost to time, her name lived on in the hearts and minds of all who heard her story, a reminder that sometimes, the greatest adventures are the ones we find when we least expect them.

10. סיפור הגולם מפראג

בלב העיר העתיקה פראג, בתקופה של רדיפות ותלאות לקהילה היהודית, התגורר רב נערץ בשם יהודה לו בן בצלאל. הידוע בחוכמתו העמוקה ואמונתו הבלתי מעורערת, הרב לאו היה אהוב על עמו ומוערך על ידי כל מי שהכיר אותו.

כאשר הקהילה היהודית התמודדה עם איומים ואלימות הולכים וגוברים מצד שכניהם, הרב לו גדל דאגה עמוקה לשלומם. נחוש להגן על עמו מפני פגיעה, הוא פנה לתורת הקבלה העתיקה - ענף מיסטי של המיסטיקה היהודית - להדרכה.

בהסתמך על הידע שלו על הטקסטים הקדושים וכוח ההתערבות האלוהית, הרב לו יצר דמות מתנשאת מחימר והביא אותה לחיים באמצעות השם הסודי של אלוהים. דמות זו, המכונה גולם, הייתה ישות בעלת עוצמה ועוצמה עצומה, שנוצרה כדי להגן על הקהילה היהודית מפני אויביה.

כשהגולם לצידו, הצליח הרב לו להדוף התקפות ולהגן על עמו מפגיעה, להחדיר פחד במי שביקשו להזיק ולהבטיח את שלומם מול המצוקה.

אבל ככל שחלף הזמן, כוחו של הגולם החל לגדול בלתי נשלט, והרב לאו הבין שהוא לא יכול לשלוט יותר ביצור שהביא לחיים. מחשש להשלכות יצירתו, קיבל הרב לאו את ההחלטה הקשה להשבית את הגולם, להחזירו למצבו חסר חיים ולאטום אותו בעליית הגג של בית הכנסת.

האגדה מספרת שהגולם של פראג עדיין רדום עד היום, ומחכה שיקראו לו שוב בשעת הצורך הגדול ביותר של העם היהודי. ולמרות שמעשיו של הרב לו נולדו מתוך רצון להגן על קהילתו, סיפורו משמש כסיפור אזהרה על הסכנות של התעסקות בכוחות שאינם בשליטתנו.

סיפור הגולם של פראג הועבר לדורותיו, ומשמש כתזכורת לחוזק ולחוסן המתמשך של העם היהודי מול מצוקות, ולחשיבות השימוש בחוכמה ושיקול דעת בחתירה לצדק ולהגנה.

Translation:

The Tale of the Golem of Prague

In the heart of the ancient city of Prague, during a time of great persecution and hardship for the Jewish community, there lived a revered rabbi named Judah Loew ben Bezalel. Known for his deep wisdom and unwavering faith, Rabbi Loew was beloved by his people and respected by all who knew him.

As the Jewish community faced increasing threats and violence from their neighbors, Rabbi Loew grew deeply concerned for their safety. Determined to protect his people from harm, he turned to the ancient teachings of Kabbalah—a mystical branch of Jewish mysticism—for guidance.

Drawing upon his knowledge of the sacred texts and the power of divine intervention, Rabbi Loew crafted a towering figure out of clay and brought it to life using the secret name of God. This figure, known as a golem, was a being of immense strength and power, created to defend the Jewish community from their enemies.

With the golem by his side, Rabbi Loew was able to ward off attacks and protect his people from harm, instilling fear in those who sought to do them harm and ensuring their safety in the face of adversity.

But as time passed, the golem's power began to grow uncontrollable, and Rabbi Loew realized that he could no longer control the creature he had brought to life. Fearing the consequences of his creation, Rabbi Loew made the difficult decision to deactivate the golem, returning it to its lifeless state and sealing it away in the attic of the synagogue.

Legend has it that the golem of Prague still lies dormant to this day, waiting to be called upon once again in the hour of the Jewish people's greatest need. And though Rabbi Loew's actions were born out of a desire to protect his community, his story serves as a cautionary tale of the dangers of tampering with forces beyond our control.

The tale of the Golem of Prague has been passed down through generations, serving as a reminder of the enduring strength and resilience of the Jewish people in the face of adversity, and the importance of using wisdom and discernment in the pursuit of justice and protection.

Top of Form

Bottom of Form

11. גילוי קללות עתיקות

בלב ירושלים, שם מתפתלים רחובות עתיקים כמו מבוך, גרה ארכיאולוג צעיר בשם שרה. שרה הייתה על סף תגלית פורצת דרך - חדר נסתר שלפי שמועות מכיל חפצים בעלי משמעות היסטורית עצומה.

ככל ששרה התעמקה במחקר שלה, היא הלכה ונאכלה מהמסתורין סביב החדר. לחישות קללות ושומרים עתיקים נפוצו בין המקומיים, והוסיפו לתככים ולסכנה שבחיפושיה.

שרה לא נרתעה מהאזהרות, נעזרה בעמיתה, דניאל, ארכיאולוג עמית עם נטייה להרפתקה. יחד, הם יצאו למסע מסוכן ברחובות המבוכים של ירושלים, בעקבות רמזים ופענוח טקסטים עתיקים בחיפוש אחר החדר החמקמק.

אבל כשהם התקרבו למטרה שלהם, התרחשויות מוזרות החלו להטריד את מסעם. דמויות מסתוריות ארבו בין הצללים, התבוננו בכל תנועה שלהן, ולחישות מטרידות הדהדו בין הסמטאות העתיקות.

למרות אי הנוחות ההולכת וגוברת, שרה ודניאל המשיכו הלאה, מונעים על ידי צימאונם לגילוי והבטחה לגלות את סודות העבר. אבל כשהם הגיעו לבסוף לחדר הנסתר, הם נתקלו במראה מעבר לסיוטים הפרועים ביותר שלהם.

החדר לא היה מלא באוצרות עתיקים כפי שקיוו, אלא בחושך וייאוש. חפצים מקוללים עיטרו את הקירות, כוחם נובע מכוח מרושע, והילה מבשרת רעות הייתה תלויה כבדה באוויר.

כשהבינו מאוחר מדי את הסכנה שהם שחררו, שרה ודניאל נרתעו להימלט מהחדר, ליבם פועם מפחד. אבל כשהם נמלטו לתוך הלילה, הם ידעו שהם העירו בלי משים כוחות שאינם בשליטתם - ושהמסתורין האמיתי של החדר רק מתחיל.

Translation:

Unearthing Ancient Curses

In the heart of Jerusalem, where ancient streets wind like a labyrinth, there lived a young archaeologist named Sarah. Sarah was on the cusp of a groundbreaking discovery—a hidden chamber rumored to contain artifacts of immense historical significance.

As Sarah delved deeper into her research, she became increasingly consumed by the mystery surrounding the chamber. Whispers of curses and ancient guardians circulated among the locals, adding to the intrigue and danger of her quest.

Undeterred by the warnings, Sarah enlisted the help of her colleague, Daniel, a fellow archaeologist with a penchant for adventure. Together, they embarked on a perilous journey through the labyrinthine streets of Jerusalem, following clues and deciphering ancient texts in search of the elusive chamber.

But as they neared their goal, strange occurrences began to plague their journey. Mysterious figures lurked in the shadows, watching their every move, and unsettling whispers echoed through the ancient alleyways.

Despite their growing unease, Sarah and Daniel pressed on, driven by their thirst for discovery and the promise of unlocking the secrets of the past. But when they finally reached the hidden chamber, they were met with a sight beyond their wildest nightmares.

The chamber was not filled with ancient treasures as they had hoped, but with darkness and despair. Cursed artifacts adorned the walls, their power emanating like a malevolent force, and an ominous aura hung heavy in the air.

Realizing too late the danger they had unleashed, Sarah and Daniel scrambled to escape the chamber, their hearts pounding with fear. But as they fled into the night, they knew that they had unwittingly awakened forces beyond their control—and that the true mystery of the chamber was only just beginning.

12. כשחלומות טסים

פעם בעיר התוססת חיפה, חי אמן רחוב צעיר בשם אבי. אבי נודע בציורי הקיר הצבעוניים שלו שעיטרו את חומות העיר, כל אחד מהם מספר סיפור של תקווה וחוסן.

אחר צהריים שטוף שמש אחד, כשאבי שם את הגימור ליצירת המופת האחרונה שלו, הוא הבחין בזקן סקרן שמתבונן בו מעבר לרחוב. עיניו של האיש נצצו משובבות כשהתקרב לאבי, ידיו תחובות בכיסי מעילו השנוש.

"עבודה יפה, איש צעיר," אמר הזקן, קולו מתפצפץ כמו עלי סתיו. "אבל האם אתה יודע את הכוח האמיתי של האמנות שלך?"

אבי הרים גבה, מסוקרן מדבריו הנסתרים של הזקן. "למה את מתכוונת?" הוא שאל.

הזקן רכן קרוב, נשימתו מדיפה ריח מנטה ומסתורין. "אני אגלה לך סוד קטן," הוא לחש. "לציורי הקיר שלך יש את הכוח להתעורר לחיים."

אבי לעג לדבריו של הזקן, ופטר אותם כקשקושים של משוגע. אבל כשחזר לציור הקיר שלו, הוא לא הצליח להשתחרר מתחושת הסקרנות שכרסמה בו.

באותו לילה, כשאבי שכב במיטה, הוא מצא את עצמו לא מצליח לישון. דברי הזקן הדהדו במוחו, ומילאו אותו בתחושת פליאה ואפשרות. האם זה יכול להיות נכון? האם האמנות שלו באמת יכולה להתעורר לחיים?

כשהוא לא יכול לעמוד בפני פיתוי האלמוני, חמק אבי מהמיטה וחזר לרחוב בו ניצב ציור הקיר שלו. ביד מהוססת, הוא הושיט את ידו ונגע במשטח המצויר, עצם את עיניו ורצה שהיצירה שלו תתעורר לחיים.

לתדהמתו, ציור הקיר החל לנצנץ ולהתהפך, צבעיו רוקדים לאור הירח. ואז, לנגד עיניו, הדמויות שצייר קמו לחיים, יצאו מהקיר אל העולם.

לבו של אבי דפק בהתרגשות כשהתבונן ביצירותיו חוקרות את העיר, וצחוקן מהדהד ברחובות. בפעם הראשונה, הוא הבין את הכוח האמיתי של האמנות שלו - להביא שמחה וקסם לאלו שהיו עדים לכך.

מאותו יום ואילך, ציורי הקיר של אבי הפכו ליותר מסתם ציורים - הם הפכו לפורטלים לעולם אחר, שבו חלומות ומציאות משתלבים זה בזה בשטיח של צבע ופליאה. ובעודו צפה באנשי חיפה מתפעלים מיצירותיו, אבי ידע שגילה את מטרתו האמיתית - לצייר עולם שבו הכל אפשרי.

Translation:

When Dreams Take Flight

Once upon a time in the vibrant city of Haifa, there lived a young street artist named Avi. Avi was known for his colorful murals that adorned the walls of the city, each one telling a story of hope and resilience.

One sunny afternoon, as Avi was putting the finishing touches on his latest masterpiece, he noticed a curious old man watching him from across the street. The man's eyes twinkled with mischief as he approached Avi, his hands tucked into the pockets of his threadbare coat.

"Beautiful work, young man," the old man said, his voice crackling like autumn leaves. "But do you know the true power of your art?"

Avi raised an eyebrow, intrigued by the old man's cryptic words. "What do you mean?" he asked.

The old man leaned in close, his breath smelling of peppermint and mystery. "I'll let you in on a little secret," he whispered. "Your murals have the power to come to life."

Avi scoffed at the old man's words, dismissing them as the ramblings of a madman. But as he turned back to his mural, he couldn't shake the feeling of curiosity that gnawed at him.

That night, as Avi lay in bed, he found himself unable to sleep. The old man's words echoed in his mind, filling him with a sense of wonder and possibility. Could it be true? Could his art truly come to life?

Unable to resist the lure of the unknown, Avi slipped out of bed and returned to the street where his mural stood. With a hesitant hand, he reached out and touched the painted surface, closing his eyes and willing his creation to come alive.

To his astonishment, the mural began to shimmer and shift, its colors dancing in the moonlight. And then, before his very eyes, the characters he had painted came to life, stepping out of the wall and into the world.

Avi's heart raced with excitement as he watched his creations explore the city, their laughter echoing through the streets. For the first time, he realized the true power of his art—to bring joy and magic to those who witnessed it.

From that day forward, Avi's murals became more than just paintings—they became portals to another world, where dreams and reality intertwined in a tapestry of color and wonder. And as he watched the people of Haifa marvel at his creations, Avi knew that he had discovered his true purpose—to paint a world where anything was possible.

13. מתחת לגלים

בעיירת החוף נתניה, השוכנת בין מימי הים התיכון התכולים לחולות הזהובים של החוף, התגורר דייג צעיר בשם יוסי. יוסי בילה את כל חייו על הים, הטיל את הרשתות שלו עם עלות השחר וחזר עם המלכוד שלו בשעת בין ערביים.

יום אחד, כשיוסי יצא על הסירה שלו לדוג, הוא הבחין במשהו מנצנץ מתחת לגלים - דג זהוב מסתורי, קשקשיו זורחים כמו השמש. מסוקרן מהמראה, יוסי הושיט את ידו לתפוס אותו, אבל הדג חמק בין אצבעותיו ונעלם במעמקים למטה.

נחוש בדעתו ללכוד את הדג החמקמק, בילה יוסי ימים בסריקת הים, והטיל את הרשתות שלו בחיפוש אחר היצור המנצנץ. אבל לא משנה כמה הוא ניסה, הדג תמיד הצליח להתחמק ממנו, חמק כמו חלום חולף.

מתוסכל ומותש, התחיל יוסי לאבד תקווה לתפוס אי פעם את דג הזהב. אבל בדיוק כשעמד לוותר, שמע קול קורא לו ממעמקי הים.

"יוסי, אל תתייאש", אמר הקול. "אני שומר הים, וצפיתי בך בעניין רב. אתה מחפש את דג הזהב, אבל אתה לא מבין שערכו האמיתי לא טמון ביופיו, אלא בשיעורים שהוא יכול ללמד אותך."

בנחישות מחודשת, הקשיב יוסי כששומר הים העניק את חוכמתו, לימד אותו לכבד את האוקיינוס ואת כל יצוריו. וכפי שלמד, התחיל יוסי לראות את הים באור חדש, לא כמקום של שפע אינסופי, אלא כמערכת אקולוגית עדינה שיש להגן ולהוקיר.

מאותו יום ואילך, יוסי כבר לא חיפש את דג הזהב, כי הוא הבין שערכו האמיתי טמון בשיעורים שהוא לימד אותו. וכשהפליג בים, שיתף את החוכמה החדשה שלו עם כל מי שהיה מקשיב, והפך לא רק לדייג, אלא לשומר הים בזכות עצמו.

Translation:

Beneath the Waves

In the coastal town of Netanya, nestled between the azure waters of the Mediterranean Sea and the golden sands of the shore, there lived a young fisherman named Yossi. Yossi had spent his entire life on the sea, casting his nets at dawn and returning with his catch at dusk.

One day, as Yossi set out on his boat to fish, he noticed something glimmering beneath the waves—a mysterious golden fish, its scales shining like the sun. Intrigued by the sight, Yossi reached out to catch it, but the fish slipped through his fingers and disappeared into the depths below.

Determined to capture the elusive fish, Yossi spent days scouring the sea, casting his nets in search of the shimmering creature. But no matter how hard he tried, the fish always managed to evade him, slipping away like a fleeting dream.

Frustrated and exhausted, Yossi began to lose hope of ever catching the golden fish. But just when he was about to give up, he heard a voice calling out to him from the depths of the sea.

"Yossi, do not despair," the voice said. "I am the guardian of the sea, and I have watched you with great interest. You seek the golden fish, but you do not realize that its true value lies not in its beauty, but in the lessons it can teach you."

With renewed determination, Yossi listened as the guardian of the sea imparted his wisdom, teaching him to respect the ocean and all its creatures. And as he learned, Yossi began to see the sea in a new light, not as a place of endless bounty, but as a delicate ecosystem that must be protected and cherished.

From that day forward, Yossi no longer sought the golden fish, for he understood that its true worth lay in the lessons it had taught him. And as he sailed the seas, he shared his newfound wisdom with all who would listen, becoming not just a fisherman, but a guardian of the sea in his own right.

14. סיפור על גילוי וידידות

פעם, בכפר מוזר השוכן בהרי הגליל, גרה ילדה צעירה בשם מרים. מרים נודעה ברחבי הכפר בחביבותה ובאהבתה להרפתקאות. מדי יום, היא הייתה חוקרת את השבילים המתפתלים שחצו את האזור הכפרי, רוחה הסקרנית הובילה אותה לתגליות חדשות.

בוקר שטוף שמש אחד, כשמרים יצאה להרפתקה היומית שלה, היא נתקלה בנתיב נסתר שמעולם לא הבחינה בו. מסוקרנת, היא עקבה אחר השביל עמוק יותר לתוך היער, אור השמש מנומר מבעד לעלים שמעל.

תוך כדי הליכה שמעה מרים את צליל הקלוש של מוזיקה מרחפת על הרוח. סקרנית היא עקבה אחרי המנגינה המלודית עד שהגיעה לקרחת יער ביער, שם מצאה קבוצת ילדים רוקדת וצוחקת מסביב לבמה מאולתרת.

במרכז הבמה עמד נער צעיר עם שיער פרוע ועיניים כחולות בוהקות, מפרט בגיטרה ושר בקול שנראה מהדהד בין העצים. מהופנטת מהמוזיקה, מרים התקרבה, לבה פועם בהתרגשות.

הילד הרים את מבטו וראה את מרים עומדת בקצה הקרחת. בחיוך חם, הוא סימן לה קדימה, והזמין אותה להצטרף לריקוד. בלי היסוס עלתה מרים לבמה, רגליה נעות בקצב המוזיקה כשהיא מסתובבת ומסתובבת עם שאר הילדים.

כשהשמש שקעה מתחת לאופק והכוכבים החלו לנצנץ בשמי הלילה, המוזיקה התפוגגה והותירה אחריה רק קול צחוק ורשרוש עלים. מרים חייכה, חשה תחושת שמחה ושייכות שלא הכירה מעולם.

מאותו יום ואילך, מרים חזרה לקרחת היער בכל פעם שהייתה זקוקה לרגע של שלווה ואושר. ובכל ביקור היא גילתה פלאים חדשים ורכשה חברים חדשים, רוח ההרפתקנות שלה הובילה אותה לאינספור מסעות גילוי.

אבל בתוך הצחוק והמוזיקה, מרים מעולם לא שכחה את הלקח שלמדה באותו יום - שלפעמים, ההרפתקאות הגדולות ביותר הן אלו שאנו מוצאים כשהכי פחות מצפים להן, מוסתרות בפינות השקטות של ליבנו.

Translation:

A Tale of Discovery and Friendship

Once upon a time, in a quaint village nestled in the hills of Galilee, there lived a young girl named Miriam. Miriam was known throughout the village for her kindness and her love of adventure. Every day, she would explore the winding paths that crisscrossed the countryside, her curious spirit leading her to new discoveries.

One sunny morning, as Miriam set out on her daily adventure, she stumbled upon a hidden path that she had never noticed before. Intrigued, she followed the path deeper into the forest, the sunlight dappling through the leaves overhead.

As she walked, Miriam heard the faint sound of music floating on the breeze. Curious, she followed the melodic tune until she reached a clearing in the forest, where she found a group of children dancing and laughing around a makeshift stage.

At the center of the stage stood a young boy with tousled hair and bright blue eyes, strumming a guitar and singing with a voice that seemed to echo through the trees. Mesmerized by the music, Miriam stepped closer, her heart pounding with excitement.

The boy glanced up and caught sight of Miriam standing at the edge of the clearing. With a warm smile, he beckoned her forward, inviting her to join the dance. Without hesitation, Miriam stepped onto the stage, her feet moving to the rhythm of the music as she twirled and spun with the other children.

As the sun dipped below the horizon and the stars began to twinkle in the night sky, the music faded away, leaving only the sound of laughter and the rustling of leaves in its wake. Miriam smiled, feeling a sense of joy and belonging that she had never known before.

From that day forward, Miriam returned to the forest clearing whenever she needed a moment of peace and happiness. And with each visit, she discovered new wonders and made new friends, her adventurous spirit leading her on countless journeys of discovery.

But amidst the laughter and the music, Miriam never forgot the lesson she had learned that day—that sometimes, the greatest adventures are the ones we find when we least expect them, hidden away in the quiet corners of our own hearts.

Top of Form

Bottom of Form

15. מעבר לדף: האודיסאה של הסופר

בעיר השוקקת תל אביב, בתוך ההמולה של חיי היום יום, גרה כותבת ספרים מתבודדת בשם רחל. רייצ'ל הייתה ידועה בסיפוריה הכובשים שהרחיקו את הקוראים לארצות רחוקות ולמחוזות קסומים, אך למרות הצלחתה, היא העדיפה את הבדידות השקטה של דירתה הנעימה.

ימיה של רייצ'ל היו שקועים בכתיבתה, תוך כתיבה של סיפורי הרפתקאות ורומנטיקה עד מאוחר בלילה. אבל למרות התפוקה הפורה שלה, היא חשה כמיהה סודית למשהו נוסף - כמיהה לחוות את ההרפתקאות עליהן כתבה ממקור ראשון.

יום אחד, כשדפדפה בחנות ספרים ישנה בלב העיר, נתקלה רייצ'ל בסיפור מאובק שהוחבאה על מדף נשכח. מסוקרנת, היא פתחה את הספר והחלה לקרוא, מאבדת את עצמה בין דפיו כשהמילים העבירו אותה לעולם של קסם ופליאות.

כשרחל התעמקה בספר, היא הרגישה תחושה מוזרה שוטפת אותה - עקצוץ בקצות אצבעותיה ורפרוף בחזה. ואז, בהבזק של אור, היא מצאה את עצמה עומדת בעיצומו של העולם שעליו היא קראה - עולם של אבירים ודרקונים, של טירות וממלכות.

בהתחלה, רייצ'ל התמלאה בפחד ובחוסר ודאות, לא בטוחה איך הגיעה למקום המוזר הזה. אבל כשחקרה את סביבתה, היא הבינה שניתנה לה הזדמנות נדירה לחיות את ההרפתקאות שתמיד חלמה עליהן.

באומץ מחודש, רייצ'ל יצאה למסע לחשוף את המסתורין של הממלכה הקסומה הזו, כשבדרך נתקלה ביצורים מיתיים ואבירים אצילים. ועם כל הרפתקה חדשה, היא מצאה השראה לכתיבתה, ושזרה את סיפורי החוויות שלה לתוך הסיפורים שכתבה.

אבל כשמסעה של רייצ'ל התקרב והיא התכוננה לחזור לעולמה שלה, היא הבינה שההרפתקאות שלה השתנתה לנצח. כבר לא הסתפקה בכתיבה פשוטה על פלאי העולם, היא השתוקקה לחקור אותם בעצמה, לחוות את הריגוש שבגילוי ואת השמחה שבהתחלות חדשות.

וכך, בלב מלא הכרת תודה ובמוח שופע השראה, נפרדה רחל מהתחום הקסום וחזרה לתל אביב, מוכנה לצאת לפרק חדש בהרפתקה משלה - ההרפתקה של לחיות את החיים במלואם, סיפור אחד בכל פעם.

Translation:

Beyond the Page: The Writer's Odyssey

In the bustling city of Tel Aviv, amidst the hustle and bustle of everyday life, there lived a reclusive bookwriter named Rachel. Rachel was known for her captivating stories that whisked readers away to far-off lands and enchanted realms, but despite her success, she preferred the quiet solitude of her cozy apartment.

Rachel's days were spent immersed in her writing, penning tales of adventure and romance late into the night. But despite her prolific output, she harbored a secret longing for something more—a yearning to experience the adventures she wrote about firsthand.

One day, while browsing through an old bookstore in the heart of the city, Rachel stumbled upon a dusty tome hidden away on a forgotten shelf. Intrigued, she opened the book and began to read, losing herself in its pages as the words transported her to a world of magic and wonder.

As Rachel delved deeper into the book, she felt a strange sensation wash over her—a tingling in her fingertips and a fluttering in her chest. And then, in a flash of light, she found herself standing in the midst of the very world she had been reading about—a world of knights and dragons, of castles and kingdoms.

At first, Rachel was filled with fear and uncertainty, unsure of how she had come to be in this strange place. But as she explored her surroundings, she realized that she had been given a rare opportunity to live out the adventures she had always dreamed of.

With newfound courage, Rachel embarked on a quest to uncover the mysteries of this magical realm, encountering mythical creatures and noble knights along the way. And with each new adventure, she found inspiration for her writing, weaving the tales of her own experiences into the stories she penned.

But as Rachel's journey drew to a close and she prepared to return to her own world, she realized that she had been forever changed by her adventures. No longer content to simply write about the wonders of the world, she longed to explore them for herself, to experience the thrill of discovery and the joy of new beginnings.

And so, with a heart full of gratitude and a mind brimming with inspiration, Rachel bid farewell to the magical realm and returned to Tel Aviv, ready to embark on a new chapter of her own adventure—the adventure of living life to the fullest, one story at a time.

16. שלושת החזירים הקטנים

פעם, ביער שופע ומוריק, חיו שלושה חזירים קטנים בשם פיגי, וויגי וזיגי. לכל חזיר היו אישיות וחלומות ייחודיים משלו, אבל הם חלקו קשר עמוק כאחים.

פיגי, הצעיר בשלישייה, היה מלא באנרגיה חסרת גבול וסקרנות אינסופית. הוא לא אהב יותר מאשר להשתובב בשמש, לרדוף אחרי פרפרים ולהסתובב בעשב הרך. כשהגיע הזמן לבנות את ביתו, פיגי בחר באפשרות המהירה והקלה ביותר - קש. אחרי הכל, חשב, מה יכול להיות נעים יותר מבית עשוי קש?

וויגי, החזיר האמצעי, היה קצת יותר זהיר ומעשי. הוא העריץ את רוחו חסרת הדאגות של אחיו פיגי אך גם הבין את חשיבות הביטחון והיציבות. כשהגיע הזמן לבנות את ביתו, וויגי בחר במקלות חזקים, מתוך אמונה שהם חזקים מספיק כדי לעמוד בכל אתגר שיקרה בדרכם.

זיגי, הבכור מבין השלושה, היה ידוע בחוכמתו ובראיית הנולד שלו. הוא תמיד היה האחראי, דאג לאחיו הצעירים והדריך אותם בסבלנות עדינה. זיגי ידע את הערך של עבודה קשה והתמדה, והוא היה נחוש לבנות בית שיעמוד במבחן הזמן. עם תכנון קפדני ותשומת לב קפדנית לפרטים, זיגי בנה את ביתו מלבנים מוצקות, בטוח ביכולתו להגן על משפחתו מכל סכנה.

כשהימים הפכו לשבועות והשבועות לחודשים, שלושת החזירים הקטנים התיישבו בבתיהם, כל אחד גאה בעבודת כפיו ולהוט להתחיל את חייהם החדשים ביער.

אבל מעט הם ידעו, זאב ערמומי וערמומי ארב בין הצללים, עיניו נוצצות מרעב כשהתבונן בחזירים הולכים בשגרת יומם. הזאב חשק זה מכבר את המנות הטעימות שחיו ביער, והוא ראה בשלושת החזירים הקטנים את ההזדמנות המושלמת לספק את התיאבון הרעבן שלו.

יום אחד, בזמן שיצא לטיול ביער, פיגי נתקל באחו יפהפה מלא בפרחי בר ופרפרים. נפעם מהיופי של הסצנה, הוא איבד את תחושת הזמן ועד מהרה מצא את עצמו רחוק מהבית, בלי שום מושג איך לחזור.

כשהערב התקרב והיער החשיך, פיגי הבין את טעותו והחל להיכנס לפאניקה. הוא מעולם לא נעדר מאחיו זמן רב כל כך, והמחשבה לבלות את הלילה לבדו ביער מילאה אותו פחד.

בינתיים, בבתיהם, וויגי וזיגי גדלו ומודאגים כאשר פיגי לא הצליח לחזור. הם חיפשו גבוה ונמוך, קראו בשמו וסרקו כל סנטימטר ביער, אבל לא היה שום סימן לאחיהם.

בדיוק כשהם עמדו לוותר על התקווה, שמעו רשרוש חלש בשיחים הסמוכים. כשתחושת הקלה שוטפת אותם, הם מיהרו לעבר הצליל, ליבם פועם בציפייה.

ושם, הגיח מהצללים, היה פיגי - מלוכלך, פרוע, אבל ללא פגע. עם דמעות של שמחה זולגות על פניהם, וויגי וזיגי חיבקו את אחיהם, אסירי תודה על כך שהוא חוזר בריא ושלם.

אבל שמחתם הייתה קצרת מועד, שכן בחושך מאחוריהם ארב הזאב, עיניו נוצצות מרעב כשהתבונן בשלושת החזירים הקטנים מתאחדים. בנהמה מאיימת הוא צעד קדימה, שיניו החדות חשופות וטפריו ערוכים להתקפה.

אבל שלושת החזירים הקטנים לא עמדו לרדת ללא קרב. עם נחישות עזה בוערת בליבם, הם התאגדו יחד, עומדים כתף אל כתף כשהם מתמודדים עם אויבם המפחיד.

וכשהזאב זינק קדימה, לסתותיו נסגרות בשאגה מחרישת אוזניים, שלושת החזירים הקטנים עצמו את עיניהם ונרתמו לפגיעה - רק כדי לפתוח אותם שוב ולמצוא את עצמם עומדים בביטחון של בית הלבנים שלהם, יללות התסכול של הזאב מהדהד מרחוק.

שכן בית הלבנים החזק של זיגי עמד חזק מול ההסתערות הבלתי פוסקת של הזאב, וסיפק מחסה והגנה לאחיו בשעת צרה. וכשהם הצטופפו יחד בפנים, בריאים ושלמים שוב, ידעו שלושת החזירים הקטנים שלא משנה אילו אתגרים צפויים להם, הם יתמודדו איתם יחד, מאוחדים בקשר האהבה והמשפחה שלהם.

Translation:

The Three Little Pigs

Once upon a time, in a lush and verdant forest, there lived three little pigs named Piggie, Wiggie, and Ziggy. Each pig had their own unique personality and dreams, but they shared a deep bond as siblings.

Piggie, the youngest of the trio, was full of boundless energy and endless curiosity. He loved nothing more than frolicking in the sunshine, chasing butterflies, and rolling around in the soft grass. When it came time to build his house, Piggie opted for the quickest and easiest option—straw. After all, he reasoned, what could be cozier than a house made of straw?

Wiggie, the middle pig, was a bit more cautious and practical. He admired his brother Piggie's carefree spirit but also understood the importance of security and stability. When it came time to build his house, Wiggie chose sturdy sticks, believing them to be strong enough to withstand any challenge that came their way.

Ziggy, the eldest of the three, was known for his wisdom and foresight. He had always been the responsible one, looking out for his younger brothers and guiding them with gentle patience. Ziggy knew the value of hard work and perseverance, and he was determined to build a house that would stand the test of time. With careful planning and meticulous attention to detail, Ziggy constructed his house out of solid bricks, confident in its ability to protect his family from any danger.

As the days turned into weeks and the weeks turned into months, the three little pigs settled into their respective homes, each one proud of their handiwork and eager to begin their new lives in the forest.

But little did they know, a crafty and cunning wolf lurked in the shadows, his eyes gleaming with hunger as he watched the pigs go about their daily routines. The wolf had long coveted the tasty morsels that lived in the forest, and he saw the three little pigs as the perfect opportunity to satisfy his voracious appetite.

One day, while out on a stroll through the forest, Piggie happened upon a beautiful meadow filled with wildflowers and butterflies. Entranced by the beauty of the scene, he lost track of time and soon found himself far from home, with no idea how to get back.

As evening approached and the forest grew dark, Piggie realized his mistake and began to panic. He had never been away from his brothers for so long, and the thought of spending the night alone in the forest filled him with fear.

Meanwhile, back at their homes, Wiggie and Ziggy grew increasingly worried when Piggie failed to return. They searched high and low, calling out his name and scouring every inch of the forest, but there was no sign of their brother.

Just as they were about to give up hope, they heard a faint rustling in the bushes nearby. With a sense of relief washing over them, they rushed towards the sound, their hearts pounding with anticipation.

And there, emerging from the shadows, was Piggie—dirty, disheveled, but unharmed. With tears of joy streaming down their faces, Wiggie and Ziggy embraced their brother, grateful to have him back safe and sound.

But their joy was short-lived, for lurking in the darkness behind them was the wolf, his eyes gleaming with hunger as he watched the three little pigs reunite. With a menacing growl, he stepped forward, his sharp teeth bared and his claws poised for attack.

But the three little pigs were not about to go down without a fight. With a fierce determination burning in their hearts, they banded together, standing shoulder to shoulder as they faced down their fearsome foe.

And as the wolf lunged forward, his jaws snapping shut with a deafening roar, the three little pigs closed their eyes and braced for impact—only to open them again and find themselves standing in the safety of their brick house, the wolf's howls of frustration echoing in the distance.

For Ziggy's sturdy brick house had stood strong against the wolf's relentless onslaught, providing shelter and protection for his brothers in their time of need. And as they huddled together inside, safe and sound once more, the three little pigs knew that no matter what challenges lay ahead, they would face them together, united in their bond of love and family.

17. עץ הזית הקסום

בלב כפר ציורי השוכן בין הגבעות המתגלגלות של ישראל העתיקה, גרה נערה צעירה בשם שירה. בעיניה הבוהקות ובצחוק המדבק, שירה הייתה תענוג הכפר, אהובה על כל מי שהכיר אותה. היא בילתה את ימיה בחקר הכפר השופע, התפעלה מהיופי של הטבע וחלמה על הרפתקאות גדולות.

אחר צהריים קיץ חמים אחד, תוך כדי שיטוט בין מטעי הזיתים שהקיפו את כפרה, נתקלה שירה במראה שעצר את נשימתה. בין שורות עצי הזית המסוקסים ניצבה דגימה מפוארת שלא דומה לאף אחת שראתה אי פעם. ענפיו נמתחו גבוה אל השמים, מטילים צללים מנומרים על האדמה מתחת, ועליו נצצו בזוהר קסום שנראה כאילו רוקדים באור השמש.

מסוקרנת מיופיו של העץ, שירה ניגשה אליו בזהירות, לבה פועם בהתרגשות. כשהושיטה את ידה לגעת בגזע שלה, קול עמוק ומהדהד הדהד דרך החורשה, וגרם לעלים לרשרוש ולענפים להתנדנד.

"מי מעז להפריע את תרדמת עץ הזית הקסום?" הקול הוסיף.

נבהלת אך לא נרתעת, שירה עמדה על שלה, עיניה פעורות בפליאה. "אני שירה, כפרית צנועה מהעיר הסמוכה", היא ענתה, קולה רועד קלות. "אני מתכוון לא להזיק, עץ אצילי. אני רק מבקש להעריץ את היופי שלך וללמוד מחוכמתך."

לרגע השתררה דממה, נשברה רק על ידי רשרוש עדין של העלים ברוח. ואז, לתדהמתה של שירה, העץ החל לדבר פעם נוספת, קולו התמלא בעוצמה עמוקה ועתיקת יומין.

"יש לך לב טהור, שירה, ורוח מלאה בסקרנות", רעם העץ. "אני חש פוטנציאל גדול בתוכך, ניצוץ של קסם המשתוקק להשתחרר. כפרס על טוב לבך, אעניק לך שלוש משאלות. אבל בחר בחוכמה, כי אין להקל ראש בקסם של עץ הזית. "

המומה מהתרגשות והכרת תודה, הרהרה שירה במשאלותיה בזהירות, מוחה דוהר באפשרויות. היא חשבה על משפחתה, על חבריה ועל הכפר שלה, והיא ידעה בדיוק מה היא הכי רוצה.

למשאלתה הראשונה ביקשה שירה אספקה אינסופית של זיתים כדי להאכיל את המשפחות הרעבות בכפר שלה. העץ הנהן באישור ובגל ענפיו הרעיף על שירה סלסלות גדושות זיתים שמנמנים ובשלים, ריחם העשיר ממלא את האוויר במתיקות.

למשאלתה השנייה ביקשה שירה להגן על עץ הזית מפגיעה כדי שיוכל להמשיך ולפרנס את כפרה לדורות הבאים. שוב, העץ נענה לבקשתה, והקיף את עצמו במחסום בלתי חדיר של קסם כדי להרחיק כל מי שיבקש לפגוע בו.

לבסוף, למשאלתה השלישית, ביקשה שירה את החוכמה לדעת איך להשתמש במתנות החדשות שלה למען שיפור הקהילה שלה. העץ חייך לחכמתה והעניק לה את הידע שחיפשה, ממלא את לבה ומוחה בחוכמת הדורות.

כשרצונותיה נענו ולבה מלא הכרת תודה, נפרדה שירה מעץ הזית הקסום וחזרה לכפר שלה, שם שיתפה את קסם המפגש שלה עם כל מי שהיה מקשיב. הזיתים סיפקו הזנה ומזון לתושבי הכפר, והחוכמה שצברה שירה עזרה לה להפוך למנהיגה ומדריכה לקהילה שלה.

ולמרות שחלפו שנים רבות ושירה הזדקנה, קסמו של עץ הזית התקיים, עדות לכוח החסד, הנדיבות והרוח המתמשכת של עם ישראל.

Translation:

The Magic Olive Tree

In the heart of a picturesque village nestled among the rolling hills of ancient Israel, there lived a young girl named Shira. With her bright eyes and infectious laughter, Shira was the delight of the village, loved by all who knew her. She spent her days exploring the lush countryside, marveling at the beauty of nature and dreaming of grand adventures.

One warm summer afternoon, while wandering through the olive groves that surrounded her village, Shira stumbled upon a sight that took her breath away. Amidst the rows of gnarled olive trees stood a magnificent specimen unlike any she had ever seen before. Its branches stretched high into the sky, casting dappled shadows upon the ground below, and its leaves shimmered with a magical glow that seemed to dance in the sunlight.

Intrigued by the tree's beauty, Shira approached it cautiously, her heart pounding with excitement. As she reached out to touch its trunk, a deep, resonant voice echoed through the grove, causing the leaves to rustle and the branches to sway.

"Who dares to disturb the slumber of the Magic Olive Tree?" the voice intoned.

Startled but undeterred, Shira stood her ground, her eyes wide with wonder. "I am Shira, a humble villager from the nearby town," she replied, her voice trembling slightly. "I mean no harm, noble tree. I only seek to admire your beauty and learn from your wisdom."

For a moment, there was silence, broken only by the gentle rustling of the leaves in the breeze. Then, to Shira's amazement, the tree began to speak once more, its voice filled with a deep and ancient power.

"You have a pure heart, Shira, and a spirit filled with curiosity," the tree rumbled. "I sense great potential within you, a spark of magic that yearns to be unleashed. As a reward for your kindness, I shall grant you three wishes. But choose wisely, for the magic of the olive tree is not to be taken lightly."

Overwhelmed with excitement and gratitude, Shira pondered her wishes carefully, her mind racing with possibilities. She thought of her family, her friends, and her village, and she knew exactly what she desired most.

For her first wish, Shira asked for an endless supply of olives to feed the hungry families in her village. The tree nodded in approval and, with a wave of its branches, showered Shira with baskets overflowing with plump, ripe olives, their rich scent filling the air with sweetness.

For her second wish, Shira asked for the olive tree to be protected from harm so that it could continue to provide for her village for generations to come. Once again, the tree granted her request, surrounding itself with an impenetrable barrier of magic to ward off any who would seek to harm it.

Finally, for her third wish, Shira asked for the wisdom to know how to use her newfound gifts for the betterment of her community. The tree smiled at her wisdom and bestowed upon her the knowledge she sought, filling her heart and mind with the wisdom of the ages.

With her wishes granted and her heart full of gratitude, Shira bid farewell to the Magic Olive Tree and returned to her village, where she shared the magic of her encounter with all who would listen. The olives provided nourishment and sustenance to the villagers, and the wisdom Shira gained helped her to become a leader and mentor to her community.

And though many years passed and Shira grew old, the magic of the olive tree lived on, a testament to the power of kindness, generosity, and the enduring spirit of the people of Israel.

18. השביל מואר הכוכבים

בכפר ציורי השוכן בין הגבעות השופעות של ארץ ישראל העתיקה, גר נער צעיר בשם אלי. עם שיערו המעורער ועיניו הבהירות מלאות פליאה, אלי נודע בכל הכפר ברוח ההרפתקנות שלו ובסקרנותו שאינה יודעת שובע. מהרגע שהיה יכול ללכת, הוא היה משוטט בין כרי הדשא והיערות, דמיונו בוער במסתרי העולם הסובב אותו.

ערב אחד, כשאלי שוטט בכיכר הכפר, הוא הבחין בקבוצת זקנים שהתאספו סביב מדורה מהבהבת, פניהם מוארים בזוהר החם שלה. אלי מסוקרן מהמראה, ניגש אל הזקנים והקשיב בקשב רב כשדיברו על אגדה עתיקה שעברה בדורות.

"אומרים", פתח זקן אחד, קולו נדם בחרדת קודש, "שפעם בכל דור, תחת אור הירח המלא, מופיע שביל מיסטי בגבעות. שביל זה, המכונה שביל מואר כוכבים, מוביל אל עבר גן סודי שבו פורחים הפרחים הנדירים ביותר והאוצרות היקרים ביותר חבויים".

ליבו של אלי זינק מהתרגשות באזכור הרפתקה קסומה שכזו. נחוש בדעתו לחשוף את האמת מאחורי האגדה, הוא בירך את הזקנים לילה טוב ויצא לדרך אל תוך הלילה, עיניו נעוצות בכדור הזוהר של הירח המלא מעליו.

מונחה על ידי אורו האתרי של הירח, עזה אלי עמוק אל הגבעות, חושיו חיים בציפייה. בעודו מתרחק מהכפר, נראה היה שהעולם סביבו מתעורר לחיים עם אפשרות, כל צל ולחש רמזו על הנפלאות שציפו לו.

שעות חלפו כשאלי פסע בשטח המחוספס, דרכו מוארת בזוהר הרך של הירח מלמעלה. בדרך הוא נתקל באינספור מכשולים, ממצוקים נישאים ועד לסבך צפוף של עצים. אבל עם כל אתגר שעמד בפניו, הנחישות שלו רק הלכה וגברה, ניזונה מההבטחה של האוצרות שהיו לפניו.

לבסוף, כשאור השחר הראשון החל לפרוץ באופק, אלי הגיע לפסגת הגבעה הגבוהה ביותר והביט אל הנוף שמתחתיו. לתדהמתו, זוהר קלוש הופיע מרחוק, מנצנץ כמו משואה בחושך. במרץ מחודש הוא דחק קדימה, ליבו פועם בהתרגשות.

בעודו עוקב אחר הזוהה, אלי מצא את עצמו חוצה שביל צר שנחצב בצלע הגבעה, האוויר סמיך בניחוח פרחי בר וקולות של יצורים ליליים המתחילים מתרדמתם. עם כל צעד שעשה, הזוהר הלך והתבהר, והוביל אותו קרוב יותר ויותר ליעדו.

לבסוף, אחרי מה שהרגיש כמו נצח, אלי הגיח לתוך קרחת יער קטנה שטופה באור הרך של הירח. לפניו היה גן מפואה, יופיו מעבר לכל מה שאי פעם דמיין. פרחים מכל צורה וצבע פרחו בשפע, עלי הכותרת שלהם נוצצים מטל.

במרכז הגן ניצב הדום, שעליו ישב כדור יחיד וזוהר, פועם באור של אלף כוכבים. מהופנט מיופיו, אלי ניגש אל הכן והושיט יד לגעת בכדור, מרגיש את חמימותו עוטפת אותו כמו שמיכה של אור ירח.

כשהביט בכדור, אלי הרגיש תחושת שלווה שוטפת אותו, כאילו כל הדאגות והדאגות של העולם נמסו. באותו רגע, הוא ידע שגילה משהו באמת יוצא דופן, משהו שיישאר איתו לשארית ימיו.

עם אור השחר הראשון צובע את השמיים בגוונים של ורוד וזהב, אלי נפרד מהגן והחל את מסעו חזרה לכפר. תוך כדי הליכה, נשא עמו את זיכרון ההרפתקה שלו, תזכורת לקסם שהיה חבוי בעולם ולכוחם של האומץ, הסקרנות ואור הירח.

ולמרות שיחלפו שנים רבות ואלי יזדקן, זיכרון שביל הכוכבים יישאר חרוט בלבו לעד, עדות לרוח ההרפתקה המתמשכת שהנחתה אותו במסעו.

Translation:

The Starlit Path

In a picturesque village nestled among the lush hills of ancient Israel, there lived a young boy named Eli. With his tousled hair and bright eyes filled with wonder, Eli was known throughout the village for his adventurous spirit and insatiable curiosity. From the moment he could walk, he would wander through the meadows and forests, his imagination ablaze with the mysteries of the world around him.

One evening, as Eli roamed the village square, he noticed a group of elders gathered around a flickering fire, their faces illuminated by its warm glow. Intrigued by the sight, Eli approached the elders and listened intently as they spoke of an ancient legend passed down through generations.

"It is said," one elder began, his voice hushed with reverence, "that once every generation, under the light of the full moon, a mystical path appears in the hills. This path, known as the Starlit Path, leads to a secret garden where the rarest flowers bloom and the most precious treasures are hidden."

Eli's heart leaped with excitement at the mention of such a magical adventure. Determined to uncover the truth behind the legend, he bid the elders goodnight and set off into the night, his eyes fixed on the glowing orb of the full moon overhead.

Guided by the moon's ethereal light, Eli ventured deep into the hills, his senses alive with anticipation. As he journeyed further from the village, the world around him seemed to come alive with possibility, each shadow and whisper hinting at the wonders that awaited him.

Hours passed as Eli trekked through the rugged terrain, his path illuminated by the soft glow of the moon above. Along the way, he encountered countless obstacles, from towering cliffs to dense thickets of brambles. But with each challenge he faced, his determination only grew stronger, fueled by the promise of the treasures that lay ahead.

Finally, as the first light of dawn began to break on the horizon, Eli reached the summit of the tallest hill and gazed out upon the landscape below. To his amazement, a faint glow appeared in the distance, shimmering like a beacon in the darkness. With renewed vigor, he pressed forward, his heart pounding with excitement.

As he followed the glow, Eli found himself traversing a narrow path carved into the side of the hill, the air thick with the scent of wildflowers and the sounds of nocturnal creatures stirring from their slumber. With each step he took, the glow grew brighter, guiding him ever closer to his destination.

At last, after what felt like an eternity, Eli emerged into a small clearing bathed in the soft light of the moon. Before him lay a magnificent garden, its beauty beyond anything he had ever imagined. Flowers of every shape and color bloomed in abundance, their petals glistening with dew.

In the center of the garden stood a pedestal, upon which sat a single, radiant orb, pulsing with the light of a thousand stars. Mesmerized by its beauty, Eli approached the pedestal and reached out to touch the orb, feeling its warmth envelop him like a blanket of moonlight.

As he gazed upon the orb, Eli felt a sense of peace wash over him, as if all the cares and worries of the world had melted away. In that moment, he knew that he had discovered something truly extraordinary, something that would stay with him for the rest of his days.

With the first light of dawn painting the sky in shades of pink and gold, Eli bid farewell to the garden and began his journey back to the village. As he walked, he carried with him the memory of his adventure, a reminder of the magic that lay hidden within the world and the power of courage, curiosity, and the light of the moon.

And though many years would pass and Eli would grow old, the memory of the Starlit Path would remain etched in his heart forever, a testament to the enduring spirit of adventure that had guided him on his journey.

19. המפתח האבוד: מסע של גילוי

בלב כפר ציורי השוכן בין הגבעות המתגלגלות של ישראל העתיקה, גר נער צעיר בשם דוד. בעיניו החדות ובסקרנותו חסרת הגבולות, דוד נודע ברחבי הכפר כרוח הרפתקנית, שתמיד להוטה לחקור את מסתורי העולם הסובב אותו.

יום גורלי אחד, כשדוד שוטט בפאתי הכפר, משך תשומת לבו לבית חווה ישן ורעוע שניצב נטוש בין העשבים הגבוהים. מסקרן את הפיתוי של המבנה הנשכח, דוד התקרב, צעדיו עוררו ענני אבק כשהתקרב.

בעודו חקר את הקירות המתפוררים וקרשים הרצפה החורקים של בית החווה, מבטו של דוד נפל על מפתח קטן ומוכתם הקבור למחצה מתחת לערימת עלים. באצבעות רועדות הוא הושיט את ידו והרים את המפתח, מתפעל מהעיצוב המורכב שלו ומתחושת ההיסטוריה שנראה שהוא נושא.

נחוש בדעתו לחשוף את התעלומה מאחורי המפתח, דייוויד יצא למסע אחר הבעלים החוקי שלו. הוא חיפש בכל פינה ופינה בכפר, ושאל שכנים וחברים אם אי פעם ראו מנעול שתואם את העיצוב הייחודי של המפתח. אבל ככל שינסה, דיוויד לא הצליח למצוא זכר למנעול שאליו הוא שייך.

לא נרתע מחוסר התשובות, החליט דוד להרחיב את חיפושיו אל מעבר לגבולות הכפר. בלי שום דבר מלבד המפתח ובנחישותו הבלתי מעורערת, הוא יצא למסע שייקח אותו הרחק מהרחובות המוכרים ואל הלא נודע.

בנסיעה על פני נופים טרשיים ודרך יערות עבותים, נתקל דוד באתגרים רבים לאורך הדרך. הוא התמודד עם סערות עזות ושטח בוגדני, נחישותו נבחנת עם כל מייל שחלף. אבל לאורך כל זה, הוא נשאר איתן במסעו, ניזון מהתקווה לחשוף את האמת מאחורי המפתח המסתורי.

כשימים הפכו לשבועות ושבועות לחודשים, מסעו של דוד הוביל אותו לארצות רחוקות ולתרבויות לא מוכרות. הוא חצה מדבריות וחצה נהרות, לבו התמלא בהתרגשות ובחשש מהצפוי למה שעומד לפניו.

לבסוף, לאחר מה שהרגיש כמו נצח של חיפושים, הגיע דוד למרגלות הר מתנשא, פסגתו אפופה בערפל ומסתורין. עם תחושת ציפייה שנבנית בחזהו, הוא החל את הטיפוס המפרך לפסגה, עיניו נעוצות באופק ככל שהוא עולה מעלה מעלה.

לבסוף, לאחר עלייה מפרכת, הגיע דוד לפסגת ההר וראה מראה שעצר את נשימתו. לפניו השתרע עמק נסתר, שופע ומוריק, יופיו ללא השוואה. ובמרכז העמק ניצבה טירה מפוארת, קירותיה מעוטרים בגילופים מורכבים ותכשיטים מנצנצים.

עם תחושת פליאה זורמת בעורקיו, ניגש דוד אל הטירה ופתח את דלתותיה העצומות. בפנים, הוא גילה אוצר שלא דומה לשום דבר שראה בעבר. זהב וכסף נצצו באור האפלולי, בעוד אבני חן יקרות נצצו במקומות מעוטרים.

אבל בין העושר, היה משהו אחר, משהו בעל ערך הרבה יותר מזהב או תכשיטים. בלב הטירה, בחדר שטוף אור זהוב, מצא דוד דלת נעולה שלא דומה לשום דלת שראה אי פעם. פני השטח שלו היו מעוטרים בסמלים מורכבים ובסימנים קודרים, המרמזים על הסודות שנמצאים מעבר.

ביד רועדת הכניס דוד את המפתח למנעול וסובב אותו, לבו הולם בחזהו כשהוא מחכה בנשימה עצורה. ולתדהמתו, הדלת נפתחה בתנופה, וחשפה חדר מלא במגילות וחפצים עתיקים, כל אחד יקר יותר מקודמו.

בעודו חקר את החדר, דוד הבין שהוא חשף ספרייה נסתרת, מאגר של ידע וחוכמה שעברו לאורך הדורות. עם כל מגילה שפרש ובכל חפץ שבדק, הוא חש תחושה של יראה ויראת כבוד כלפי ההיסטוריה והתרבות שבאו לפניו.

באותו רגע ידע דוד שהוא מצא את המטרה האמיתית של מסעו. שכן בפתיחת הדלת ובגילוי האוצרות שבתוכו, הוא פתח את הדלת לידע ולהבנה, אוצר גדול בהרבה מכל מה שיכול היה לדמיין.

עם לב מלא הכרת תודה ותחושת מטרה חדשה, חזר דוד הביתה לכפר, ומסעו הושלם לבסוף. ולמרות שאולי לעולם לא יידע את מלוא היקף התעלומות שחשף, הוא ידע שהמסע היה שווה את זה, שכן הוא גילה את האוצר הגדול מכולם: המפתח לפתיחת סודות העבר.

Translation:

The Lost Key: A Journey of Discovery

In the heart of a picturesque village nestled amidst the rolling hills of ancient Israel, there lived a young boy named David. With his keen eyes and boundless curiosity, David was known throughout the village as an adventurous spirit, always eager to explore the mysteries of the world around him.

One fateful day, as David roamed the outskirts of the village, his attention was drawn to an old, dilapidated farmhouse that stood abandoned amidst the tall grasses. Intrigued by the allure of the forgotten structure, David ventured closer, his footsteps stirring up clouds of dust as he approached.

As he explored the crumbling walls and creaking floorboards of the farmhouse, David's gaze fell upon a small, tarnished key half-buried beneath a pile of leaves. With trembling fingers, he reached out and picked up the key, marveling at its intricate design and the sense of history it seemed to carry.

Determined to uncover the mystery behind the key, David set off on a quest to find its rightful owner. He searched every nook and cranny of the village, asking neighbors and friends if they had ever seen a lock that matched the key's unique design. But try as he might, David could find no trace of the lock it belonged to.

Undeterred by the lack of answers, David resolved to expand his search beyond the boundaries of the village. With nothing but the key and his unwavering determination, he embarked on a journey that would take him far from the familiar streets and into the unknown.

Traveling across rugged landscapes and through dense forests, David encountered many challenges along the way. He faced fierce storms and treacherous terrain, his resolve tested with each passing mile. But through it all, he remained steadfast in his quest, fueled by the hope of uncovering the truth behind the mysterious key.

As days turned into weeks and weeks into months, David's journey led him to distant lands and unfamiliar cultures. He traversed deserts and crossed rivers, his heart filled with both excitement and trepidation at the prospect of what lay ahead.

Finally, after what felt like an eternity of searching, David arrived at the foot of a towering mountain, its peak shrouded in mist and mystery. With a sense of anticipation building in his chest, he began the arduous climb to the summit, his eyes fixed on the horizon as he ascended higher and higher.

At last, after a grueling ascent, David reached the summit of the mountain and beheld a sight that took his breath away. Before him lay a hidden valley, lush and verdant, its beauty beyond compare. And at the center of the valley stood a grand castle, its walls adorned with intricate carvings and shimmering jewels.

With a sense of wonderment coursing through his veins, David approached the castle and pushed open its massive doors. Inside, he discovered a treasure trove unlike anything he had ever seen before. Gold and silver gleamed in the dim light, while precious gems sparkled in ornate settings.

But amidst the riches, there was something else, something far more valuable than gold or jewels. At the heart of the castle, in a chamber bathed in golden light, David found a locked door unlike any he had ever seen before. Its surface was adorned with intricate symbols and arcane markings, hinting at the secrets that lay beyond.

With a trembling hand, David inserted the key into the lock and turned it, his heart pounding in his chest as he waited with bated breath. And to his amazement, the door swung open, revealing a chamber filled with ancient scrolls and artifacts, each one more precious than the last.

As he explored the chamber, David realized that he had uncovered a hidden library, a repository of knowledge and wisdom passed down through the ages. With each scroll he unrolled and each artifact he examined, he felt a sense of awe and reverence for the history and culture that had come before him.

In that moment, David knew that he had found the true purpose of his journey. For in unlocking the door and discovering the treasures within, he had unlocked the door to knowledge and understanding, a treasure far greater than any he could have imagined.

With a heart full of gratitude and a newfound sense of purpose, David returned home to the village, his quest finally complete. And though he may never know the full extent of the mysteries he had uncovered, he knew that the journey had been worth it, for he had discovered the greatest treasure of all: the key to unlocking the secrets of the past.

20. חוטי מורשת

בכפר הציורי אוקווד, השוכן בין גבעות מתגלגלות ויערות לוחשים, התגוררה אישה בשם מרים. מרים, שנחשבה ללב הקהילה, נודעה בהתנהגותה העדינה ובמסירותה הבלתי מעורערת לשימור מסורות אבותיה.

מגיל צעיר הייתה מרים שבויה בסיפורים שסבתה הייתה מספרת - סיפורים על ימים עברו, על תלאות שעברו ועל ניצחונות שנחגגו. היא הייתה מקשיבה בתשומת לב נלהבת כשסבתה דיברה על מסעה של המשפחה בארצות רחוקות, על המאבקים איתם התמודדו והקשרים שהחזיקו אותם יחד.

ככל שחלפו השנים, מרים מצאה את עצמה נמשכת לעליית הגג של בית אבות משפחתה, אוצר של זיכרונות שמחכים להתגלות. שם, בין האבק וקורי העכביש, היא נתקלה בתא מטען נשכח מלא עד אפס מקום בקליידוסקופ של שאריות בד. כל גרוטאה נשאה איתה פיסת היסטוריה, חוט המחבר אותה לדורות עברו.

עם גל של השראה, מרים החליטה לצאת למסע כדי לשזור את הפיסות השונות הללו לתוך שטיח זיכרון - שמיכת טלאים שתשמש עדות חיה לשטיחי הקיר העשיר של מורשת משפחתה.

מרים אספה את שאריות הבד והניחה אותם לפניה, והתחקתה אחר סיפורי אבותיה התפורים לכל חלק. היו שם דוגמיות משמלת הכלה של סבתא רבא שלה, דהויות עם הגיל אבל עדיין נושאות את ניחוח היסמין מהגן שבו החליפה נדרים. היו שרידים מהמדים הצבאיים של סבה, שנשאו סימנים של קרבות שנלחמו וניצחונות ניצחו. והיו שאריות בד מהסינר של אמה, מוכתמים בקמח מאינספור שעות בילוי במטבח, והעבירו מתכונים וחוכמה מדור לדור.

בידיים רועדות החלה מרים לחבר את שברי ההיסטוריה של משפחתה, בכל תפירה תפילה לעבר ותקווה לעתיד. ימים הפכו לשבועות, ושבועות הפכו לחודשים כשמרים עמלה ללא לאות על שמיכתה, ושופכת את לבה ונשמתה בכל תפר.

תוך כדי עבודתה, השמיכה הפכה ליותר מסתם אוסף של שאריות בדים - היא הפכה למחווה חיה לחוסן ולחוזק של אבותיה, עדות לכוח המתמשך של אהבה וחיבור.

לבסוף, לאחר אינספור שעות של עמל, מרים שמה את הליטוש האחרון ביצירת המופת שלה – שמיכת טלאים שנצצה בצבעים של אלף זיכרונות, כל חוט שזור בהקפדה ויראת כבוד.

כשהיא מציגה את יצירתה בגאווה לעיני כל, מרים הזמינה את שכנותיה וחברותיה להתאסף סביב כשהיא חולקת את הסיפורים מאחורי כל פיסת בד. וכשהם הקשיבו, גם הם הרגישו את כובד ההיסטוריה לוחץ עליהם, מחבר אותם למורשת שנמתחה לאורך הדורות.

בשנים שלאחר מכן הפכה שמיכתה של מרים לירושת אהובה, שעברה מדור לדור כסמל למשפחה, לאהבה ולכוחה המתמשך של המסורת. וכל עוד נשארה השמיכה, כך גם סיפורי אבותיה, השזורים במרקם עצמו לנצח נצחים.

Translation:

Threads of Heritage

In the picturesque village of Oakwood, nestled amidst rolling hills and whispering forests, there resided a woman named Miriam. Widely regarded as the heart of the community, Miriam was known for her gentle demeanor and unwavering dedication to preserving the traditions of her ancestors.

From a young age, Miriam had been captivated by the stories her grandmother would tell – tales of days gone by, of hardships endured and triumphs celebrated. She would listen with rapt attention as her grandmother spoke of the family's journey across distant lands, of the struggles they faced and the bonds that held them together.

As the years passed, Miriam found herself drawn to the attic of her family's ancestral home, a treasure trove of memories waiting to be discovered. It was there, amidst the dust and cobwebs, that she stumbled upon a forgotten trunk filled to the brim with a kaleidoscope of fabric remnants. Each scrap carried with it a piece of history, a thread connecting her to generations past.

With a surge of inspiration, Miriam decided to embark on a journey to weave these disparate scraps into a tapestry of remembrance – a patchwork quilt that would serve as a living testament to the rich tapestry of her family's heritage.

Gathering the fabric scraps and laying them out before her, Miriam traced the stories of her ancestors stitched into every piece. There were swatches from her great-grandmother's wedding gown, faded with age but still carrying the scent of jasmine from the garden where she had exchanged vows. There were remnants of her grandfather's military uniform, bearing the marks of battles fought and victories won. And there were scraps of fabric from her mother's apron, stained with flour from countless hours spent in the kitchen, passing down recipes and wisdom from one generation to the next.

With trembling hands, Miriam began to piece together the fragments of her family's history, each stitch a prayer for the past and a hope for the future. Days turned into weeks, and weeks turned into months as Miriam labored tirelessly over her quilt, pouring her heart and soul into every seam.

As she worked, the quilt became more than just a collection of fabric scraps – it became a living tribute to the resilience and strength of her ancestors, a testament to the enduring power of love and connection.

Finally, after countless hours of labor, Miriam put the finishing touches on her masterpiece – a patchwork quilt that shimmered with the colors of a thousand memories, each thread woven with care and reverence.

Proudly displaying her creation for all to see, Miriam invited her neighbors and friends to gather around as she shared the stories behind each piece of fabric. And as they listened, they too felt the weight of history pressing down upon them, connecting them to a legacy that stretched back through the ages.

In the years that followed, Miriam's quilt became a cherished heirloom, passed down from one generation to the next as a symbol of family, love, and the enduring power of tradition. And as long as the quilt remained, so too would the stories of her ancestors, woven into its very fabric for all eternity.

Conclusion

Learning the basics of any language is difficult, and the Hebrew language can feel daunting for many newcomers. With that being said, if you were able to finish all of the lessons in this book, you have built a solid foundation in Hebrew.

However, learning a language is a long process that rewards consistency. Even just listening and watching Hebrew shows for 30 minutes a day can go a long way in improving your Hebrew skills. We sincerely hope that you continue your Hebrew language journey with the foundation you have built up and reach your goals, whether that be to understand the basics or speak like a native.

Thank you for choosing our book along your path to Hebrew mastery and we hope that you obtained a lot of useful information! If you have any questions, comments, or even suggestions we would love to hear from you by email at Contact@worldwidenomadbooks.com. We greatly appreciate the feedback and this allows us to improve our books and provide the best language learning experience we can.

Thank you,

Worldwide Nomad Team

Made in the USA
Middletown, DE
15 February 2025

71381910R00116